CHILLING ADMISSIONS
The Affirmative Action Crisis and the Search for Alternatives

Edited by
GARY ORFIELD AND EDWARD MILLER

The Civil Rights Project, Harvard University
Harvard Education Publishing Group

Library of Congress Catalog Card Number 98-71079

ISBN 1-891792-00-8

Harvard Education Publishing Group
349 Gutman Library
6 Appian Way
Cambridge, MA 02138

Cover Design: Kate Canfield
Cover Photo: Associated Press/Lacy Atkins
Editorial Production: Dody Riggs
Typography: Sheila Walsh

Contents

v   **Acknowledgments**

vii   **Foreword**
    Christopher Edley, Jr.

CHAPTER 1
1   **Campus Resegregation and Its Alternatives**
    Gary Orfield

CHAPTER 2
17   **Misconceptions in the Debate Over Affirmative Action in College Admissions**
    Thomas J. Kane

CHAPTER 3
33   **No Alternative: The Effects of Color-Blind Admissions in California**
    Jerome Karabel

CHAPTER 4
51   ***Hopwood* in Texas: The Untimely End of Affirmative Action**
    Jorge Chapa and Vincent A. Lazaro

CHAPTER 5
71   **The *Hopwood* Chill: How the Court Derailed Diversity Efforts at Texas A&M**
    Susanna Finnell

CHAPTER 6

83   Notes from the Field: Higher Education Desegregation
in Mississippi
Robert A. Kronley and Claire V. Handley

CHAPTER 7

97   Race and Testing in College Admissions
Michael T. Nettles, Laura W. Perna, and Catherine M. Millett

CHAPTER 8

111   Testing a New Approach to Admissions: The Irvine
Experience
Susan A. Wilbur and Marguerite Bonous-Hammarth

CHAPTER 9

123   An Admissions Process for a Multiethnic Society
*Greg Tanaka, Marguerite Bonous-Hammarth, and
Alexander W. Astin*

131   About the Contributors

Acknowledgments

This is the first book from The Harvard Civil Rights Project. We are deeply indebted to the MacArthur Foundation for its initial grant, which helped launch the project, paid to commission the papers, and supported the conference that led to this book, as well as the editing process on this book. The MacArthur Foundation, together with the Mellon Foundation, provided the first significant risk capital to launch our project and make studies like this possible.

The Charles Stewart Mott and Rockefeller Foundations and an anonymous donor have provided core support for the project. The Spencer Foundation funded the first meeting of higher education and civil rights leaders, which led to our decision to organize the Civil Rights Project as a civil rights think tank.

This project could not have functioned without the extraordinary work of Michal Kurlaender, our coordinator. As a graduate student she was a wonderful volunteer. As our first—and for a long time our only—employee, she held things together and contributed in many ways to this book and to every major event of the project.

We are also deeply indebted to the Harvard Education Publishing Group, which decided to invest in this book and committed significant resources to get our publishing enterprise launched. It has been a pleasure to share this experience with them.

Foreword

June 1998 marks the 20th anniversary of the U.S. Supreme Court's decision in *Bakke,* in which the Court struck down a seemingly rigid minority set-aside in admissions at the University of California, Davis Medical School. A majority of the justices, however, agreed that universities can use race as a factor in decisionmaking in order to promote diversity in higher education, provided it is done flexibly and carefully.

Admittedly, today's legal and political climate seems increasingly in-hospitable to race-conscious affirmative action measures. (By "affirmative action" I mean the use of race or ethnicity as a factor in admissions deci-sions or the allocation of resources.) Conservative critics have been quick to announce the death knell of affirmative action whenever there is a judicial, legislative, or electoral development favoring their cause. Their messages typically come in a coordinated communications effort, giving the most dramatic possible interpretation to events. Indeed, this communication strategy has been so successful that even civil rights traditionalists occasion-ally speak of the "post–affirmative action" era.

This propaganda and defeatism, however, are both at odds with some legal and practical realities: Over these 20 years, the Supreme Court has not overruled *Bakke,* and successive generations of leaders in selective universi-ties have pursued affirmative action, believing it to be the only effective means of achieving the inclusion critical to their core missions. Like many business executives, these educators view diversity and inclusion as an ele-ment of excellence and a strategy for success. If the Supreme Court elimi-nates the diversity rationale for race-conscious measures in admissions, it will force a radical shift in public and private practices—hardly a "conserva-tive" undertaking.

This volume focuses on the following interrelated questions:[1] What would be the consequences for student body diversity of eliminating race and ethnicity as factors in university admissions? More specifically, what if we relied entirely on traditional quantitative measures of academic achieve-ment and promise, such as test scores and GPA? And, are there alternative, nonracial criteria that one might use in admissions and still do reasonably well in achieving desired levels of both diversity and academic preparedness?

The legal framework for these questions comes from the Equal Protection clause of the Fourteenth Amendment to the U.S. Constitution, and from Title VI of the Civil Rights Act of 1964.[1] It is impermissible for institutions to treat people differently based on race or ethnicity *unless* 1) there is a compelling interest and 2) the race-conscious measure is narrowly tailored. The first test, compelling interest, can be met if the university is acting to remedy the vestiges of its own racial discrimination, or racial discrimination closely associated with that institution. Achieving campus diversity is also a compelling interest, under Justice Powell's opinion in *Bakke,* as well as the widespread practice of a quarter century.

This diversity rationale, however, is under severe political and judicial attack. We see this in California's adoption of Proposition 209 in November 1996, and in the Fifth Circuit's decision in *Hopwood,* which effectively gutted *Bakke* for Texas, Mississippi, and Louisiana. The central question is this: Are the benefits to be achieved from inclusion substantial enough to be a compelling interest in constitutional terms, as well as desirable social policy in the broader sense? The answer, which is the subject of the second volume in this series, is critical to the public and judicial deliberations on the diversity rationale and the survival of *Bakke.*

Also critical to America's deliberations, however, are the questions in this volume. In legal parlance, the matter of nonracial alternatives is within the "narrow tailoring" prong of the constitutional analysis. After all, if there are nonracial means of pursuing an admittedly compelling interest, it makes sense to use those less troubling tools. Presumably, however, these nonracial tools must have some reasonable likelihood of effectiveness. The Supreme Court has not required that decisionmakers wear rose-colored glasses, or assume that heaven has come to earth. A practical inquiry is necessary. Facts matter.

In the policy and political arena, the analysis of nonracial alternatives is similarly critical. When President Clinton announced his "mend it, don't end it" policy in July 1995, he also stressed that decisionmakers should use workable alternatives where they exist. Some institutions face politically imposed, legislated, or judicial restrictions (under *Hopwood*) on race-conscious measures, making a consideration of nonracial strategies imperative.

This collection of papers does not address in great detail one of the most common nonracial alternatives: fixing the K-12 pipeline, which civil rights conservatives argue is an adequate substitute for affirmative action in university admissions. Proponents of affirmative action also support improving elementary and secondary education, but insist that instead of "either-or," it must be "both-and." They question the strength, effectiveness, and timeliness of these pipeline strategies.

Separate-but-equal was embraced by some as an equal opportunity strategy, but in fact it was not. *Brown v. Board of Education* could have been implemented as an effective pipeline improvement strategy, but it wasn't. Title I funding for remedial education could have been a powerful tool to repair the pipeline, but that promise, too, has dimmed. Mentoring and partnership programs are now all the rage, but there is as yet no evidence of their systemic effectiveness.

Strategies and slogans come and go, but genuinely equal opportunity remains elusive, if not illusory. The heart of the case for diversity-based affirmative action in admissions (and employment, too) is this: While the struggle to repair the pipeline continues toward uncertain and perhaps distant success, we cannot allow the nation's leading institutions to undermine their educational and social missions by excluding capable underrepresented minorities. They must not return to their 1950 demographics while the face of 21st-century America becomes so radically different.

It is important, in the midst of controversy, that neither universities nor civil rights advocates be complacent. "Mend it, don't end it" is a good slogan. But it also captures the constitutional requirement of narrow tailoring, and expresses the political and ethical imperatives of due care when adopting and executing affirmative practices.

Within all of this turmoil, no one should rush to assume that nonracial alternatives will do the job well enough. The analyses collected in this volume provide strong evidence that they will not. Judges and educators must not blithely assume, for example, that class-based affirmative measures alone will enable selective institutions to fulfill their missions. On the other hand, educators and policy leaders must not assume that the general public will defer to the judgments of elite academics.

Preserving affirmative action will require investigation of and relentless teaching about the benefits of inclusion, the likely failings of nonracial alternatives, and the continuing need for careful affirmative action, until educational opportunity is truly equal.

Perhaps analysis can be an antidote to propaganda and defeatism. And perhaps facts can help prevent a headlong, ill-founded rush to throw out effective affirmative action measures and replace them with alternatives that are likely to fail.

CHRISTOPHER EDLEY, JR.
Professor of Law, Harvard Law School
Codirector, The Civil Rights Project

Note

[1] The Equal Protection clause applies to governmental actors. Title VI extends the same basic anti-discrimination principles to private entities receiving federal funds; it covers virtually every private college and university because of federal student aid and research grant programs.

CHAPTER 1

Campus Resegregation and Its Alternatives

GARY ORFIELD

After a generation of serious efforts by U.S. colleges and universities to reverse their historic exclusion of African Americans, Latinos, and American Indians, these institutions are suddenly facing a frontal attack on the programs, policies, and commitments born of those efforts. Threatened by court decisions, referenda, political attacks, and lawsuits, colleges are struggling to foresee the consequences of abandoning affirmative action and to devise viable alternatives for promoting and preserving campus diversity. This volume documents and examines that struggle.

As the communities around them become more and more diverse, many campuses that have been forced to end affirmative admissions are now rapidly turning whiter. There are fewer minority applicants, and those who are admitted often choose to go elsewhere rather than face severe isolation. These changes can create a vicious circle of resegregation. Denying the benefits of a college education to groups that are destined to become the majority in many cities and states raises explosive issues. The first troubling examples are already evident. At the leading public law schools in Texas and California, states where the majority of students are now Latino or black, the enrollment of blacks and Latinos has dropped dramatically: the University of Texas (UT) Law School's entering class in fall 1997 was less than 1 percent black; in California black enrollment dropped by 63 percent while Latino enrollment was down by 34 percent.

The U.S. Supreme Court's 1978 decision in *Regents of the University of California v. Bakke* permitted colleges to consider race as one of a variety of factors in admissions, but forbade the use of racial quotas. The key opinion, by Justice Lewis Powell, cited Harvard University's multidimensional admissions process, which seeks to promote diversity of many kinds.

1

The rate of access to college for black high school graduates relative to whites had reached its peak just before *Bakke*, because of a variety of trends in the 1960s and early 1970s. These included a vast expansion of federal aid for low-income college students; the rapid growth of low-cost four-year state colleges; and programs from the War on Poverty, such as Upward Bound, designed to identify promising low-income students and give them both training in key pre-collegiate skills and support in preparing for and applying to college. *Bakke* enabled colleges wanting to maintain a significant minority presence to do so even as these anti-poverty programs were dismantled in the 1980s, and in spite of continuing large gaps in the preparation of minority students.

Under *Bakke,* colleges were allowed to work out something short of a quota that would boost minority access. There were few legal or political challenges to these affirmative admissions programs for a generation, while public debate focused on more visible issues such as school busing, racially defined voting districts, and affirmative action in employment. The conflicts over race on campus were about curriculum, harassment, racially defined housing and educational programs, and faculty recruitment. The few researchers who concentrated on these issues gave most attention to the problems of minority students on predominantly white campuses.

Everything changed suddenly in 1996, when federal courts of appeals in Texas and California, the two largest states, outlawed race-conscious college admissions policies. Several other states were affected by a third appeals court decision in Maryland that prohibited racially targeted financial aid. The U.S. Supreme Court, which had already limited race-conscious remedies in minority contracting, voting rights, and school desegregation, refused to hear any of these three key cases, thus effectively limiting the *Bakke* principle in large parts of the country.

As this book is published, legislative and legal challenges to affirmative admissions have been launched in several other states. Lawyers are advising some institutions to cut back on their existing admissions policies, and minority scholarships are being terminated in a number of states. In response, civil rights groups are attacking the use of standardized tests and seeking other basic changes in college admissions policies.

Higher education is fundamentally different from other civil rights arenas. Civil rights policies are usually challenged by institutions that are being forced to pursue racial goals they oppose. Most affirmative admissions and aid policies, on the other hand, are purely voluntary efforts to achieve goals the colleges themselves support. Outside the South, colleges have not faced court orders or federal sanctions to force them to admit minority students; even in the South, there has been little such enforcement. The great majority of colleges want to maintain their civil rights policies. But white students and right-wing legal action groups trying to impose a change on these institutions are asking federal courts to prohibit these voluntary efforts and prescribe different admissions policies.

In the states most affected thus far, minority communities are reacting with shock and anger. Some campuses have erupted in protests of the sort not seen since the Vietnam War. A college education has become a central part of the American dream; slamming shut the gates of college and professional school clearly threatens the future of the communities affected. But high-pitched demands for action can lead legislatures and academic administrators to consider any alternative that sounds plausible.

Education leaders and policymakers face a difficult challenge. The courts are increasingly responsive to white claims of racial discrimination while dismissing minority concerns over the continuing effects of historic discrimination. Many campuses are therefore trying to figure out how to maintain diversity without any explicit consideration of race in admissions. It would be simple if race were simply a proxy for other conditions, but, as the research in this volume shows, it is not. Race overlaps with class, educational, and job inequality, and with geographic isolation, giving rise to the hope that one or more of those factors might be an easy substitute. But race in truth is unique in its significance and impact, both historic and contemporary.

It is also true that any overt effort to specify a set of multiple factors that are obviously intended to duplicate the effect of racial selection would be seen as defiance of the court orders, because institutions may not do by subterfuge what they are prohibited from doing directly. In this complex situation, policymakers are likely to adopt new strategies that sound as if they might work with little or no serious analysis of their viability or educational consequences. Such decisions often have unanticipated consequences. If a policy turns out to be based on unworkable premises, it could discredit the goal.

For example, if a new admissions policy succeeds in admitting many minority students with far weaker preparation than those admitted under the old policy, universities would temporarily maintain minority enrollment levels but would find themselves flunking out a growing percentage of minority students unless they mounted a massive remediation effort. Because highly selective schools have few instructors skilled in remedial work and give no rewards for such work, major problems would be likely.

Moreover, Stanford Professor Elizabeth Cohen and others have shown that race relations are improved when there is equal status interaction—that is, when racial differences are not reinforced by class differences and very large achievement differences. Admitting only very poor black or Latino students from very weak schools would tend to reinforce racial stereotypes and diminish the probability of positive interracial contacts. It would be better for developing positive race relations and reducing stereotypes to find a way to admit those minority students most ready for college work.

When race-conscious admissions policies are outlawed, the easiest alternative for colleges seeking to admit significant numbers of minorities is to target high-poverty, low-achieving schools, because very few whites attend such schools. But the students from these schools will also be the least likely to succeed in college. It is extremely difficult to identify, using only nonracial criteria, those African-American and Latino applicants most likely to succeed in a selective college, because they are often middle-class students attending more competitive, less impoverished schools. (These students, of course, still face a variety of obstacles related to historic and current forms of discrimination—obstacles that opponents of affirmative action simply deny.)

The problem is complex: any purely voluntary affirmative admissions program must produce good enough results to maintain the support, or at least the acceptance, of the faculty and administration. If the policy does not work it may be terminated at any point, leaving no policy at all and fostering a belief that there is no feasible solution. It is very important, in other words, that new policies be likely to work.

Many university leaders have strongly reaffirmed their belief that maintaining campus diversity is crucial. But belief is not enough. These leaders must be prepared both for the coming legal challenges and for the possibility that they will find their accustomed authority in these matters suddenly limited. What they will need, first of all, is much better information on the likely consequences of policy alternatives. One goal of this book is to provide that information.

The Rise and Fall of Affirmative Admissions

U.S. college campuses historically reflected the dominant groups in American society, choosing students with no interference from federal courts or agencies. There were, of course, pressures from trustees, alumni, sports teams, fund-raisers, and contributors to admit certain students. Most students were white Protestant males from more affluent and educated families. Nineteen states maintained racially separate public campuses for black and white students, and seventeen (where the large majority of blacks lived) had mandatory segregation laws until 1954. Even after the Supreme Court outlawed public school segregation, very little changed until the late 1960s.

Selective colleges historically tended to reflect the biases of the larger society, including anti-Semitism and racism. Even at the few northern colleges that admitted significant numbers of black graduate students before the civil rights era, discrimination was often overt. The University of Chicago, for example, segregated its student housing and participated in a campaign to keep its neighborhood all-white through restrictive real-estate covenants.

Things began to change after World War II, when the G.I. Bill brought hundreds of thousands of less affluent students to campus. Soon the United States began a huge expansion of higher education. During the 1960s and 1970s, state and federal governments tried to make some kind of college education possible for anyone who could benefit from it. Financial aid programs were created; the War on Poverty encouraged the poor to attend college; and civil rights laws directly challenged the tradition of racial exclusion. This revolution began to open the door to white colleges for blacks.

Affirmative policies for student recruitment, admissions, and aid were important elements of this effort. Given the unequal educational backgrounds of minority students, the history of unconstitutional segregation, the continued existence of segregated and unequal public schools, the huge gaps in test scores, and the failure of limited efforts in the preceding decade to significantly integrate elite colleges and universities, many institutions devised much more focused race-conscious policies in the late 1960s and early 1970s. The basic lesson of the first decade of civil rights policymaking was that the problems were systemic: they would tend to be self-perpetuating even when overt racial barriers fell. Real change, therefore, would mean prying open the doors through a conscious plan to overturn long-standing traditions.

Those policies were often attacked as government-imposed quotas, but they were actually voluntary goals. The government could have used its authority under the 1964 Civil Rights Act to force change, but it did not. That law forbade discrimination in institutions receiving federal aid and gave the Department of Education authority to regulate institutions on issues of nondiscrimination. Even after the Office for Civil Rights was ordered by federal courts to require equity and desegregation plans in the states that had intentionally segregated students, it never used its power to cut off funds against those falling far short of their goals for minority access. In the rest of the nation, there were no regulations and no required plans for racial equity. The one major enforcement case developed in the 1970s, against the University of North Carolina, was quickly dropped when President Reagan took office.

interesting?

Ironically, probably the most aggressive investigation of admissions issues was by the Reagan administration on behalf of Asian-American students who complained that an increased emphasis on verbal skills at the University of California (UC) at Berkeley would result in the admission of fewer Asians. Under threat, the university backed down. No similar threat regarding admissions or tests that have the effect of reducing enrollment has ever been made on behalf of black, Latino, or American Indian students. Many states, in fact, have recently adopted higher admissions requirements with disproportionate negative impact on these minorities.

Most colleges and universities devised their own policies for their own reasons. The urban upheavals of the 1960s and the assassination of Martin Luther King, Jr., lent urgency to these efforts, and fostered the belief that colleges should try to develop interracial leadership for the future good of society. Colleges exercised their traditional discretion in admissions, and their authority under *Bakke*, to devise policies and practices that would identify, admit, and assist larger numbers of minority students.

Even at its peak, this effort at equity fell far short of reflecting the nation's overall population or its population of high school graduates. It came closest to equalizing rates of college entrance among white and black high school graduates in the late 1970s, just before *Bakke* and the rapid tuition increases and aid cuts of the 1980s. But there was always a large gap in graduation rates. By the early 1980s, there was a serious drop in the percentage of minority students entering college compared to whites, a racial gap that grew during the decade.

Access to college for minority families was threatened on a number of fronts. Cutbacks in state and federal funding and huge rises in tuition compounded the impact of sharp cuts in the buying power of the largest aid program, the Pell grants. The Reagan administration loosened civil rights requirements and called for the raising of entrance requirements. It also mounted an all-out attack on race-conscious civil rights remedies, announcing that states need not achieve the racial goals set for their higher education systems—even those states that had never desegregated their institutions. The administration asked the courts to permit race-based remedies only where clear discrimination was proved and, even then, only for a few years. Where there was no overt historic discrimination, it argued, no affirmative policies should be allowed because they would amount to discrimination against whites. Presidents Reagan and Bush went on to appoint the majority of all sitting federal judges; the courts increasingly leaned toward their limited vision.

By the late 1990s, this view had reshaped the law of affirmative action in employment, voting rights, minority contracting, and school desegregation. In each case the Supreme Court restrained the lower federal courts, turning authority over to state and local officials. As court-imposed remedies were terminated, the courts became more responsive to claims that even voluntary race-conscious efforts discriminated against whites. The recent appeals courts' decisions in Texas, California, and Maryland clearly reflect this transformation.

When Admissions Are Driven by Tests and Grades

Once affirmative action was stripped away in the two largest states, the consequences of ranking applicants by standardized tests became much more obvious. The studies included in this volume confirm reports from several highly selective campuses and professional schools: under the new rules there have been devastating declines in the admission of underrepresented minority students. And a recent California study suggests that, even without the use of standardized tests, differences in grades alone would produce major drops in the enrollment of black and Latino students.

Dropping racial targeting will have similar effects nationwide—particularly at the 20 percent of U.S. colleges with genuinely selective admissions—given the existing gaps in test scores and grades between whites and underrepresented minorities. Thomas Kane of Harvard's Kennedy School of Government analyzes the probable impact of such a change on the fortunes of white applicants, compared with general public perceptions of affirmative action. Because there are far more whites in the pool of eligible applicants at selective schools, Kane reasons, a drastic reduction in the number of minorities admitted would produce only a small increase in the acceptance rates of whites and Asians. At Harvard College, for instance, even if no blacks or Latinos were admitted at all, a white or Asian applicant's chances of acceptance would rise by only one or two percent. "If more than one or two percent of those who were originally denied admission believe that they would have been admitted but for affirmative action," Kane writes, "then the perceived costs of the policy overstate the true cost."

Kane's analysis illuminates a fallacy in the thinking of many critics of affirmative action, who exaggerate its actual impact and thus play on the resentment of whites who are inclined to blame it for their own disappointments. Reversing affirmative action will cause substantial harm to minority group representation on selective campuses and deepen minority skepticism about the possibility of racial progress, and yet help few whites or Asians.

The end of affirmative action on key selective campuses will reverberate throughout the educational system. Jerome Karabel of Berkeley reports that restricting enrollment of Mexican Americans in the UC and UT systems would gravely affect Latino medical school applications nationwide. Thus the entire country's supply of Latino doctors could be harmed by policy changes at just two large state university systems. From these and other data, Karabel concludes that the demise of affirmative action will mean "a return to a level of racial and ethnic segregation in American higher education not seen in more than a quarter of a century." The American Medical Association reports that minority applications to medical school fell by 11 percent in 1997.

Ending affirmative action not only limits admission to higher education but also sends a much broader signal to minority groups, who are especially sensitive to symbols. In a racially polarized society, minorities watch closely for signs of hope or of reversal. When they see what seem to be unmistakable signs that doors are being closed, many decide that they will not be allowed in. So even before the new admissions policies took effect in Texas and California, there were sharp drops in the numbers of inquiries and applications from minorities. Susanna Finnell's study of Texas A&M University documents a dramatic decline in applications from Latinos and blacks for its academic scholarships following the news that the court had outlawed affirmative action. At the same time, there was a surge of applications from whites and Asians—perhaps reflecting their overestimate of the impact of affirmative action on their groups.

Texas A&M's academic scholarships are reserved for students with high SAT or ACT scores who are also in the top segment of the graduating class. These scholarships were originally designed in part to recruit talented minority students, who are underrepresented on campus. In the year after the Texas court of appeals decision, applications for the scholarships from Latinos dropped by 36 percent; applications from blacks dropped 71 percent. The number of white applicants went up 103 percent.

Elementary and secondary public school enrollment in Texas is now 53 percent nonwhite. If current trends continue, Latinos will be the majority group in the state's public schools within a few years, but they will be largely excluded from its selective colleges.

Finnell describes Texas A&M's efforts to attract minority students to its historically white campus in recent years, including a highly effective invitational summer program targeted at talented minority youth. With such racially targeted recruitment efforts now illegal in Texas, if the university wants to continue the program it must open it to whites, quintupling its size and defeating its purpose. The result is that no one is invited. An effort to overcome a campus's historic image of racial bias through personal visits is simply abandoned. This outcome only reinforces problems rooted in a history of discrimination.

Will Race-Blind Alternatives Work?

Faced with catastrophic declines in black and Latino enrollment, policy-makers and advocates in Texas and California have begun a hurried search for race-blind alternatives that seem likely to preserve some degree of diversity on campus.

Because the courts have forbidden only the consideration of race, and because affirmative action arises from notions of redressing disadvantage, people naturally think of different definitions of disadvantage that might work. The one most often discussed in affirmative action debates is poverty, because blacks, Latinos, and American Indians are much more likely than whites to be poor. They are also likely to attend segregated, high-poverty schools.

But using poverty as a proxy for race will not preserve diversity, as analyses by Kane and Karabel show. Most poor people in the United States are neither black nor Latino, and many of the minority students admitted to college through race-conscious affirmative action are not poor. A ranking of students below the poverty line by their test scores would result in a pool of favored applicants that was mostly Asian and white—many of them from temporarily poor families who managed to send their children to competitive schools that prepared them for college entrance exams.

Recent immigrants from Asia, for example, often are highly educated people who cannot practice their professions in the United States, at least until they receive a new certification; their children, however, have the immense advantage of the parents' education and often are able to attend suburban schools because they face less housing discrimination than blacks or Latinos. The stereotype that Asian children encounter in these schools is generally positive, not negative. A policy that gives preferential admissions to such students, who enjoy family and school advantages and have experienced little discrimination in the United States, while excluding minorities who face serious discrimination, would have serious unanticipated consequences. (Some Asian refugee groups do not, of course, enjoy these advantages and in fact face problems much more like those confronting Latinos.)

To maintain the current level of black and Latino representation through preferences based on poverty instead of race, selective colleges would have to reserve six times as many places for poor students as they currently reserve for underrepresented minorities, according to Kane's analysis. Few, if any, colleges could afford to pursue such a course.

One seemingly easy but race-blind way to insure some minority representation would be to target high-poverty schools. Very few white students attend such schools; schools in which more than 90 percent of the students are black or Latino are 16 times as likely as mostly white schools to have a majority of poor kids. It is not surprising, then, that the Texas legislature, seeking a way to preserve minority access to college, fixed on this solution. It declared that the top 10 percent of students in every high school are eligible for admission to the University of Texas. This approach includes high-poverty schools in the admissions pool, using traditional measures of achievement within the school, not race, to select individual students.

Segregation is widespread but far from absolute in Texas schools, and so there is no guarantee that the top-scoring students even in heavily non-white schools will be African American or Latino. But a serious problem arises from the strikingly unequal preparation of this cohort of students.

College admissions officers have long known that class rank is hardly comparable from one high school to the next. The top students in many high-poverty schools are woefully unprepared for college. Ignoring this fact and admitting these students presents universities with a difficult choice. If nothing else changes, many of the new students will simply flunk out and the policy will be discredited. To avoid this outcome, colleges will have to invest in effective remedial strategies, something selective campuses have been notoriously reluctant to do. Many, in fact, have raised their admissions requirements in recent years and cut back remedial programs. Thus, a seemingly simple solution has the unintended effect of excluding many of the best-prepared minority students and requiring other complex changes in policy.

The assault on affirmative action has brought into much sharper focus the social consequences of relying on standardized tests in the college admissions process. Black, Latino, and American Indian students have always fared poorly on such tests. The reasons for their poor performance are complex and not entirely understood. What is clear, however, is that if colleges are forced into a slavish adherence to cutoff scores in admitting applicants, the numbers of blacks, Latinos, and American Indians on campus will fall precipitously. The enrollment figures in California and Texas law and business schools have already sparked intense scrutiny of the validity and predictive power of admissions tests, and testing policies have become principal targets of civil rights advocates.

Tests are often assumed to be neutral and highly reliable measures of merit, but experts have long known that they have large margins of error in assessing any individual student, and that their overall predictive power accounts for only a modest portion of the variance in achievement among first-year college students. Given the difficulties of choosing among thousands of similar applicants, it is easy to understand why colleges rely on an indicator that helps even a little, provides very simple, easily interpreted data, and shifts the costs to the students. As the power of tests increases, however, advocates are calling for changes in the nature and uses of those tests. A university committee in California has recommended dispensing with standardized testing entirely. Others call for the construction of different kinds of assessment that are more related to actual performance on the job, or that reflect more of the talents and experiences of minority students. Some California campuses tried to do this.

Following the court decisions ending affirmative action in Texas and California, the Texas state legislature responded to large initial losses by trying to preserve minority access by providing automatic access to the university for any student finishing in the top 10 percent of his or her high school class. University of California campuses had to admit at least half of their students purely on the basis of test scores and grades; since many applicants had perfect or near-perfect grades, the test scores alone would be decisive for them. The California campuses tried to come up with a number of other measures and procedures to address other forms of disadvantage. The most selective California campuses, however, experienced drastic declines in African American, Latino, and American Indian students.

The total of African Americans, Latinos, and American Indian undergraduates admitted at Berkeley fell from 23 percent to 10 percent, and from 20 percent to 13 percent at UCLA—this at a time when the state's minority population was rapidly rising. In Texas, in spite of the 10 percent plan, fewer blacks were admitted at Austin, and there was no increase in the number of Latinos. The group that benefited most from the 10 percent plan was Asians, who had not suffered from the end of affirmative action. At the University of Texas at Tyler, less than 15 percent of the students admitted under the 10 percent plan were minorities. The net effect was that there was no recovery from the dramatic declines that occurred following the circuit court ruling in *Hopwood v. Texas*. Schools in both states often mentioned the severe problems they had faced in recruiting those students who were admitted, caused by ending minority scholarships. Eligible black and Latino students had to consider whether or not to accept less financial aid, and whether to attend schools where they would be more isolated due to greatly reduced enrollment of minority students.

These issues will be addressed in detail in a future volume from the Harvard Civil Rights Project. They already figure prominently, however, in the early reaction to post-affirmative action problems in some states. One of the many ironies of the current situation is that those most convinced that tests truly measure "merit" are creating a political climate in which tests may ultimately be downgraded in importance.

Some universities have reacted to the crisis by belatedly deciding to develop admissions policies that comply with the spirit of *Bakke*. As Jorge Chapa and Vincent Lazaro make clear in their essay in this volume, the UT Law School provided a tempting target for white litigants because its admissions procedure clearly violated the Supreme Court's *Bakke* principle—that race could be considered only as one of many variables in a complex admissions process. Too many selective public universities did not create such a process; they simply used the standard test scores and grades and added in race. The UT Law School created a "Texas Index" by combining test scores and grades, and then treated minority and white applicants differently. It was a two-factor analysis—nothing like the *Bakke* model. This meant that applicants were arrayed on a relatively simple continuum and admissions decisions were then adjusted by taking race into account as the decisive factor.

At very selective colleges where many applicants have high grades and the choice hangs on just two variables—tests scores and race—the admissions process is particularly vulnerable to challenge. Because such systems use no other cross-cutting factors, the loss of minority students can be precipitous once race is eliminated as a criterion. Certainly any campus that retains such a flawed process after the appeals court ruling in *Hopwood* is exposing itself to the maximum risk of judicial takeover of its admissions process.

Complying with the *Bakke* model is a logical but costly alternative. A study of changes in the admissions process at UC Irvine by Susan Wilbur and Marguerite Bonous-Hammarth suggests that a multidimensional system of assessing student potential can help produce a more diverse campus. They report that the new system, implemented in the wake of a UC regents' vote ending affirmative action, resulted in significant increases in the admission of black and Latino applicants above the numbers admitted through a simple formula based on tests and grades. Their study suggests that if public universities invest in admissions processes designed to assess a broader array of talents, they may be able to remain diverse. The Irvine system did this, but the campus still had substantial drops in black and Latino admissions in 1998.

Still another important way of thinking about the problem is to reconceptualize the goals of the selection process. Admissions criteria should be seen as a way to fulfill the values of the institution and to create the most effective learning community that embodies those values. Advocates of a one-dimensional "merit"-based system seem to suggest that admission to college is simply a reward for the students who are most "deserving," as measured on the scale of test scores and grades. But universities are not passive receptacles; they are dynamic communities that profoundly affect the development of students on many dimensions that are not readily quantified. The most important intellectual interactions many students ever experience take place in college—often with other students. Universities must foster the creation of knowledge and the training of leadership for the community and its professions. Because of these critical functions of universities, admissions processes reflect considerations important to the fulfillment of community as well as individual goals. This is precisely what the Supreme Court recognized in the *Bakke* case.

Gregory Tanaka, Marguerite Bonous-Hammarth, and Alexander Astin suggest in this volume that it would be appropriate for universities to make interracial experience a "plus factor" for admissions. They cite evidence that multiracial campuses offer important advantages and that creating such communities should be a fundamental goal of a university in diverse society. Their research suggests that students who bring interracial experience with them to college may be valuable assets for these institutions. Diversity by itself, without people who understand how to make it work, may confer fewer benefits and create more problems than on campuses with many such people. If it is reasonable, Tanaka and colleagues argue, to give admissions preference to student athletes on the grounds that they enhance student life and increase external support for the school, is it not also reasonable to consider experience and skills in multiracial settings an asset? Positive race relations contribute to both the productive sharing of ideas on campus and to good institutional relationships with the outside community.

There may be other legitimate considerations in admissions. Because most colleges look only at English verbal test scores, they often underestimate students who have another first language. Outside the United States, fluency in two or more languages is considered a hallmark of an educated person. In the United States, by contrast, it is rare for students to graduate from college with a working knowledge of a second language, in spite of the importance of such knowledge in a global economy. Demonstrated fluency in a second world language could well be a plus factor in admissions decisions.

Other attributes and skills directly relate to success in careers and professions and could be incorporated into the admissions process. Leadership talent, the ability to work with others, verbal confidence, resilience, perseverance in the face of setbacks, and many other qualities are valued by employers and could be considered by admissions committees. Colleges have every right to take such qualities into account.

Every crisis presents opportunities for progress. In the long run, colleges and universities must take advantage of the affirmative action crisis to sharpen and reaffirm their goals, to develop recruitment and admissions policies that look at the whole person and recognize more of the accomplishments of minority students, and to reflect critically on how better to achieve their goals after the students arrive on campus. In the short run, however, a great deal remains at risk.

Conclusion and Recommendations

The reversal of affirmative admissions in higher education can drastically reduce black, Latino, and American Indian enrollment on highly selective campuses. The increased use of tests and grades as entrance standards will tend to exacerbate the existing inequities in U.S. society. If affirmative action is outlawed nationally, as it has been in Texas, the impact on access to leading public and private universities would be enormous. Many of our most able students would find themselves on campuses overwhelmingly dominated by white and Asian students. The severe isolation characteristic of our more affluent suburbs would become the rule in the institutions that train the leaders of our society and our professions. This threatens critical educational functions of universities and their ability to fully serve their communities.

The research reported in this volume shows that there is no good substitute for affirmative admissions efforts targeted at historically excluded groups. Any substitute criteria will be likely to bypass many of the best-prepared black and Latino students, who may face many forms of racial discrimination but are neither poor nor isolated in the weakest schools.

The likely outcome of substituting poverty for race will be the admission of fewer and less-prepared black and Latino students. Therefore, the highest priorities for supporters of minority access to college should be:

- a vigorous defense of race-conscious affirmative action admissions policies that comply with *Bakke*, which rightly called for the creation of a multidimensional admissions process that takes account of a wide variety of applicants' talents;
- documentation of the academic benefits of diversity (the subject of the second volume in this series); and

- strong efforts to counter inaccurate and polarizing claims about minority admissions.

If affirmative action is struck down, universities should undertake a long-overdue examination of the entire admissions process. The same kind of narrow formulaic approach that is most likely to exclude minorities is also likely to exclude other students with talents that are not easily measured by tests and grades and, conversely, to reward students from the most affluent and educated families and communities. If colleges define "merit" as, in effect, being born into a highly educated, suburban white or Asian family and attending a highly competitive white high school, they are serving to maintain a stratified society rather than to truly reward merit and ability. As access to college becomes more and more decisive in shaping life chances, leaders of higher education have a growing responsibility to reach out for talent and make mobility possible. Universities that grafted affirmative action onto a flawed admissions process a quarter century ago now risk losing diversity unless they build a better process. Even if they eventually are successful in defending affirmative action in the Supreme Court, the radical reversals in some regions, the experiments they produce, and the legitimate criticisms of some of the existing systems all argue for change.

The essays in this book show that research can play an important role in the affirmative action debate. But far too few rigorous studies have addressed the important issues raised in the courts and in political debates. Very little previous work addressed the basic issues before the courts today; researchers could, for example, contribute important knowledge on the history of discrimination and its continuing effects, which is the strongest legal basis for race-conscious policies. Documenting the nature of the disadvantages that middle-class blacks and Latinos still face is crucial for their continued access to higher education.

The rollback of affirmative action in higher education requires all members of the university community to consider soberly a profound social change that they have hitherto taken for granted. A generation of multiracial campuses—the only such generation in U.S. history—was the product of both a great social movement and the commitment of university leaders three decades ago. Too little has been done to renew that commitment or to make the resulting levels of diversity work even better.

Now that our campuses are threatened with a return to almost total domination by the most privileged racial and ethnic communities, educational and political leaders must ask how much they value that hard-won diversity and what they are willing to do to keep it. From that debate could emerge a new understanding of common goals—and the energy to build a more democratic system for educating the future leaders of our rapidly changing society.

CHAPTER 2

Misconceptions in the Debate Over Affirmative Action in College Admissions*

THOMAS J. KANE

Introduction[1]

Admissions committees ration access to many of our nation's most selective colleges. As changes in the labor market drive up the value of a college education and the competition for admission at the most selective institutions becomes even more keen, affirmative action has become increasingly controversial, particularly at public institutions.

Nearly two decades after the U.S. Supreme Court's 1978 *Bakke* decision, we know little about the true extent of affirmative action admissions by race or ethnicity. We know even less about the impact of those policies on the careers of the affected students. Hard evidence has been difficult to obtain, primarily because many colleges guard their admissions practices closely. This paper uses longitudinal data on a sample of high school students who graduated in 1982 to shed light on three questions relevant to the current controversy:

1. What is the actual extent of affirmative action in college admissions decisions?
2. Do affirmative action policies really help the students they are meant to help?

*Much of the discussion in this chapter is drawn from Thomas J. Kane, "Racial and Ethnic Preferences in College Admissions," in *The Black-White Test Score Gap*, edited by Christopher Jencks and Meredith Phillips (Kane, in press).

3. Could colleges rely on nonracial criteria, such as income or parental education, to produce similar levels of racial diversity on selective college campuses?

In each case, the data suggest that widely held opinions about affirmative action may well be erroneous, and that these misconceptions are driving both the debate and policymakers in the wrong direction.

A Summary of the Findings

The High School and Beyond (HSB) survey began in 1980 with a sample of about 36 sophomores from each of 1,015 public and private high schools in the United States. Follow-up data were collected in 1982, 1984, 1986, and 1992.[2] Many of these students applied to the same colleges when they graduated from high school in 1982. In 1984, the respondents were asked to report their first- and second-choice colleges and whether they had been accepted at each. The HSB survey also included extensive data on the students' high school transcripts, high school activities, and standardized test scores.

These data enable us to gauge the effect of race on the likelihood of admission to various types of colleges among applicants with similar high school grades, student activities, and test scores. The HSB study is particularly well suited to gauging the long-term consequences of affirmative action policies because it included follow-up surveys through 1992, ten years after participants' high school graduation.

The experience of the class of 1982 shows that certain institutions counted race as a "plus factor" in their admissions, but that the practice was not widespread. "Elite" universities (defined here as those with average SAT scores in the top 20 percent of four-year institutions) gave African-American applicants an advantage equivalent to nearly a full point increase in high school grade-point average (on a four-point scale), or to several hundred points on the SAT. But at the less selective schools that 80 percent of all four-year college students attend, race seemed to play little, if any, role in admissions decisions.[3]

The most damning charge against affirmative action is that it does more harm than good for the intended beneficiaries, by enticing students to attend colleges where they are unprepared for the competition. Despite the high dropout rates experienced by minorities on college campuses, the evidence does not support this charge. Attending a more selective college was associated with higher bachelor's degree completion rates and higher earnings after graduation. This was true for all racial groups, even after holding constant an individual's family background and academic preparation.

Because one cannot control for all the initial differences between students in different kinds of colleges, one cannot interpret the higher completion rates and earnings of those attending more selective institutions as pure "value added." Some of the difference in earnings and completion rates between graduates of more and less selective colleges still reflects preexisting differences in academic or earnings potential. Nevertheless, there is no evidence in the HSB data to suggest that black and Hispanic students benefit less than others from attending a selective college.

Finally, so-called class-based affirmative action—based on income or parental education—would do little to cushion the impact of ending race-conscious policies, unless elite colleges dramatically reduce their reliance on high school grades and test scores. The reason is simple: although blacks and Hispanics would benefit disproportionately from any policy designed to help low-income and first-generation college students, they nevertheless represent a minority of all low-income youth and a very small minority of high-scoring low-income youth. Race-blind class-based policies alone would therefore be unlikely to produce anything like the level of racial diversity on campus that explicit race-based policies have achieved. There is an inescapable trade-off between race-blindness and diversity at selective institutions.

The Mean Test Score Fallacy

At any one college, the average SAT scores or high school grades of black and of white applicants can differ considerably. As a result, without direct knowledge of the workings of admissions committees and the weight they attach to various factors, it is impossible to infer racial preference based solely on the observed characteristics of admitted students.

Richard Herrnstein and Charles Murray, in their 1994 book *The Bell Curve,* used the differences in the average combined SAT scores of blacks and whites attending elite colleges as evidence of massive racial preference in admissions. These differences are quite large, ranging from 288 points at the University of California at Berkeley to 95 points at Harvard. On the basis of these data, Herrnstein and Murray concluded that "the edge given to minority applicants in college and graduate school is not a nod in their favor in the case of a close call, but an extremely large advantage that puts black and Latino candidates in a separate admissions competition."

But such evidence can easily be misleading, for two reasons. First, we know that there are large differences between black and white high school graduates in average scores on tests like the SAT. If high school grades, personal references, participation in co-curricular activities, and even luck affect admissions decisions, and if these factors are not perfectly correlated with SAT scores, then racial differences in the mean SAT scores of applicants will persist in attenuated form among admitted students. To take a trivial example, imagine a college that admitted a student if he or she had a combined SAT score above 1100 or if the flip of a coin turned up "heads." Such a process is obviously race-blind. But because many students would be admitted for a reason unrelated to their SAT scores (the coin flip), racial differences in mean SAT scores among applicants would be reflected among the admitted.[4]

Second, even if all students were admitted solely on the basis of SAT scores, we would still see a difference in the mean scores of admitted students, because the distribution of SAT scores above any admission threshold would be different for blacks and whites. As reported by the College Board (Ramist & Arbeiter, 1984), blacks in the high school class of 1982 represented 2 percent of those scoring over 500, 1 percent of those scoring over 600, and 0.6 percent of those scoring over 700 on the math section of the SAT. In other words, blacks are increasingly underrepresented at high test scores. A college that admitted all students with SAT math scores above 500 would thus find that blacks were more likely than whites to have scores in the 500 to 600 range, while the opposite would be true at higher ranges. The admissions process at this college, based solely on SAT scores, would be completely color-blind, and yet its black students would have lower average scores than its white students.

Measuring the Extent of Affirmative Action Admissions

How then can we try to measure the actual extent of affirmative action in admissions? Using the responses to the HSB survey, we can compare the admission rates of similar black and white students applying to certain schools. HSB included students' scores on tests during the sophomore and senior years in high school, high school grades and activities, family income, and parental education. Holding these characteristics constant enables us to estimate the effect of race and ethnicity on the likelihood of admission.

Using the mean SAT scores reported by the schools themselves, I first sorted the colleges to which HSB students applied into five equal-sized groups, or quintiles: those with mean SAT scores in the top 20 percent of all college-reported scores; those in the 20th to 40th percentile; the 40th to 60th percentile; the 60th to 80th percentile; and, finally, the bottom 20 percent. I then evaluated the marginal contribution of various student char-

TABLE 1   *The Determinants of Admission to a Four-Year College*

	Marginal Difference in Probability of Admission for the Applicant with Mean Characteristics (by Quintile of College Selectivity)				
Quintile:	Lowest	(2)	(3)	(4)	Highest
Race (White, NH Excl.):					
Black, Non-Hispanic	−.001 (.014)	−.014 (.016)	−.020 (.027)	.031 (.011)	.103 (.028)
Hispanic	.010 (.010)	.000 (.016)	−.021 (.028)	.032 (.013)	.086 (.031)
Other, Non–Hispanic	—	−.053 (.037)	−.046 (.043)	−.087 (.059)	−.067 (.040)
Academic Credentials:					
High School Academic GPA (4-point scale)	.025 (.008)	.020 (.009)	.048 (.015)	.082 (.012)	.151 (.023)
SAT Score (/100 points)	.008 (.003)	.015 (.004)	.007 (.006)	.020 (.004)	.025 (.009)
High School Activities:					
Student Government	.002 (.010)	.026 (.010)	.009 (.017)	.002 (.012)	.053 (.020)
Athletics	.016 (.010)	.002 (.011)	.016 (.014)	.004 (.011)	.006 (.020)
College Selectivity:					
College SAT (100 points)	−.026 (.013)	−.035 (.026)	−.078 (.079)	−.025 (.039)	−.165 (.018)
N:	928	991	1,070	1,097	1,696
Prob. of admission at mean X:	.978	.967	.938	.957	.812

Note: Standard errors are reported in parentheses. The effect of being "Other, Non-Hispanic" is not identified for the lowest quintile since no such students were denied admission at those schools. Probit specifications also include indicators for eight categories of family income, five categories of parental education, and eight categories of high school sample stratum. Standard errors were calculated recognizing that the errors may be correlated within colleges, using a method proposed by Huber (1967) and White (1980).

acteristics to the likelihood of admission within each group of colleges separately. These results are reported in Table 1.

The admissions process appears to vary significantly among the different groups of schools. At the least selective 60 percent of colleges, race had little effect on the likelihood of admission. The effect of grades and SAT scores was also small. Racial and ethnic differences in the probability of admission were most pronounced at the most selective colleges (the last column in Table 1). At these schools, a student with the characteristics of the average applicant was 8 to 10 percentage points more likely to be admitted if he were black or Hispanic.[5]

Further analysis of these data reveals very little evidence that colleges weighted nonracial characteristics differently for those of different races. For instance, there is little evidence that colleges weighted the SAT scores of black and Hispanic students differently from those of whites and others. Moreover, there is little evidence that colleges granted particular advantages to low-income minority youth. (In fact, there is some evidence that colleges favored higher-income blacks and Hispanics.)

Affirmative Action and Later Life Chances[6]

Critics often point to high dropout rates and low grade-point averages among minority youth as evidence that affirmative action only harms its intended beneficiaries. In a 1988 article in *The Public Interest,* for instance, John Bunzel described the poor grades and high dropout rates of students admitted under affirmative action at the University of California at Berkeley. Bunzel implied that the high dropout rate of black students was caused by affirmative action and the resulting competitive disadvantage black students faced. Herrnstein and Murray drew a similar conclusion in *The Bell Curve* (1994).

But it is possible that the minority students at Berkeley would have dropped out in large numbers no matter where they attended college. The racial differences Bunzel and other critics observed at Berkeley may not have been a result of affirmative action admissions policies, but may have simply reflected differences in academic preparation or differences in family background among the students who were admitted. In order to isolate the net effect of attending a more selective school, one must compare outcomes for similar students attending more and less selective schools.

The HSB data allow us to do so by examining differences in college grade-point average (GPA), college completion rates, and post-college income by student and college characteristics.[7] We find that black and Hispanic students' college GPAs were lower than those of other students, even after controlling for academic preparation and family background. Attending a more selective school was also associated with having a lower GPA: a 100-point increase in the college's mean SAT score was associated with a GPA .027 points lower (on a 4-point scale).

But attending a more selective college was also associated with a 3 percent *increase* in the likelihood of B.A. completion by 1992. In other words, attending a more selective school may put a student at a competitive disadvantage with his classmates, but it nevertheless is associated with improved chances of graduating. (Author's note: For more details on the analysis, please see Kane, in press.)

In an analysis of the high school class of 1972, Loury and Garman (1995) concluded that greater college selectivity was associated with higher completion rates for whites, but lower rates for blacks. In the HSB data for the class of 1982, the apparent relationship between college selectivity and B.A. completion was significantly weaker for minority youth than for others.

But this result largely reflects the unusually high completion rates for those attending historically black institutions (HBIs). The HBIs have low mean SAT scores, but have historically generated a disproportionate share of black college graduates in the United States.[8] Blacks and Hispanics who attend HBIs have completion rates 17.2 percent higher than comparable blacks in predominantly white schools of comparable selectivity. Once we take this fact into account, the relationship between college selectivity and college completion is similar for blacks and Hispanics as for others. The same is true regarding the relationship between earnings and college selectivity.[9]

I found no evidence of a racial difference in the relationship between college selectivity and college GPA, B.A. completion, or earnings. Indeed, the evidence suggests that the gains associated with attending a more selective school are, if anything, higher for those with lower test scores.

Because admissions committees at selective colleges may ferret out the most talented candidates among those with similar high school grades and test scores, it is difficult to distinguish the true "value added" of attending a more selective institution from the effects of unmeasured advantages enjoyed by students admitted to those institutions. Therefore, my estimates probably overstate the "payoffs" of college selectivity. But the results offer no reason to think that this bias is larger for minority students than for others. (In fact, one might expect the bias to be smaller for minority students if it is primarily the most selective schools that practice affirmative action.)

For both B.A. completion and later earnings, the racial difference in the payoff of college selectivity is both small and insignificant. To the extent that more selective institutions offer benefits to their students, these payoffs seem no smaller for the black and Hispanic youth who gain admission to them than for other students.

Class and Race in Affirmative Action

As political support for race-sensitive policies in college admissions has eroded, interest in "class-based" remedies has risen—primarily as a way of cushioning the impact on racial minorities of ending affirmative action.[10] Indeed, Michael Williams, the Bush administration official who opposed race-based scholarships, has suggested that "the end of racial preferences is here, but . . . with some ingenuity and creativity, America's campuses can continue to represent the wide variety that is America."

Mr. Williams is overly optimistic. Class cannot be substituted for race in affirmative action admissions without substantial effects on campus diversity. The problem is in the numbers.

Using data from the high school class of 1992, we find that blacks and Hispanics were roughly three times as likely to have incomes under $20,000 as whites and other non-Hispanics—51 percent versus 17 percent (see Table 2). Yet blacks and Hispanics represented less than half (47 percent) of the entire low-income population. The reason for the apparent paradox is that blacks and Hispanics were a minority (23 percent) of the overall population of high school graduates in 1992. Though they were more likely than whites to have low incomes, their absolute numbers still represented a minority of the total low-income population.

The paradox is even stronger when we look at youth with combined reading and math scores in the top 10 percent of their class, because blacks and Hispanics represent an even smaller share of this subgroup. Although high-scoring blacks and Hispanics in the class of 1992 were again roughly three times more likely to be low-income than high-scoring whites and other non-Hispanics (17 percent versus 6 percent), among all low-income, high-scoring youth, blacks and Hispanics were a clear minority—only one out of six (17 percent). Because blacks and Hispanics were a minority (23 percent) of all high school graduates and a very small minority (less than 7 percent) of high school graduates with high test scores, they represented a minority of most subgroups of these populations.

These numbers reveal the difficulty of using race-blind class-based preferences to produce racial diversity on campus. A college drawing from the general population would have to admit two low-income students from the overall pool of high school graduates to yield one black or Hispanic student. But most of the colleges currently practicing affirmative action are drawing from the pool of high-scoring youth, not from the general population. At such schools, the poor substitutability of class for race is likely to be even more striking. A selective college drawing from the top 10 percent of the

TABLE 2 *The Demographics of Race and Income*

Among Those Graduating from High School in 1992:
(Row Proportion) [Column Proportion]

	Blacks and Hispanics	Whites and Other Non-Hispanics	Row Total:
Income > $20,000	266,700 (.152) [.487]	1,493,100 (.848) [.825]	1,759,800 (1.000) [.747]
Income < $20,000	280,100 (.470) [.512]	316,200 (.530) [.175]	596,300 (1.000) [.253]
Column Total:	546,800 (.232) [1.000]	1,809,300 (.768) [1.000]	

Among Those Graduating from High School in 1992
Who Had Combined Reading and Math Test Scores in the Top Tenth of the Class:
(Row Proportion) [Column Proportion]

	Blacks and Hispanics	Whites and Other Non-Hispanics	Row Total:
Income > $20,000	11,800 (.061) [.828]	182,000 (.939) [.939]	193,800 (1.000) [.932]
Income < $20,000	2,400 (.173) [.172]	11,700 (.827) [.061]	14,200 (1.000) [.068]
Column Total:	14,200 (.068) [1.000]	193,800 (.932) [1.000]	

Note: Based on author's tabulation of the 1992 wave of the National Education Longitudinal Study of 1988, a panel study of eighth-grade students from 1988.

test-score distribution would have to admit six students under a low-income preference policy to yield one black or Hispanic student. In other words, if a selective college wanted to achieve substantial minority enrollment without explicitly considering race, it would have to reserve six times as many places for low-income students as it now reserves for minority students. Moreover, such an admission policy would strain a school's financial aid budget.

What Class-Based Affirmative Action Would Look Like

In this section, we use the HSB data to search for nonracial decision rules that would mimic the admission rates achieved using race at the top quintile of four-year colleges. The first column of Table 3 estimates the effect of various factors—including race—on the likelihood of admission at a top-quintile school. In the HSB sample, the apparent effect of race on the likelihood of admission was quite large after controlling for other factors—15 percentage points for black non-Hispanic youth and 11 percentage points for Hispanic youth.[11] Moreover, there is little evidence that selective colleges used information on parental income, parental education, or high school characteristics in their admissions decisions. One could not reject the hypothesis that all of the coefficients on parental education, family income, and high school characteristics were equal to zero. As reflected in the admissions decisions reported by the HSB sample, the most selective 20 percent of colleges seemed to focus on high school grades, test scores, race, and little else.

The second and third columns in Table 3 predict the results of two hypothetical admissions experiments.[12] First, we searched for the admission rule that most closely matches the admissions decisions reported by the HSB sample while satisfying two other constraints: the rule cannot be based on race, and it must preserve the same admission rates for blacks and Hispanics as observed for the HSB sample. These results are therefore similar to what an admissions director at a selective college might have found by experimenting with a range of nonracial criteria in order to maintain the existing racial diversity in the pool of students admitted under affirmative action. The only difference is that we sought out the rule that comes closest to matching the actual decisions colleges made using race as a factor.

These results are reported in the second column of Table 3. They show what might happen if colleges tried to maintain racial diversity using the nonracial criteria of family income, parental education, and high school characteristics: they would have to reduce the likelihood of admission of those with incomes between $25,000 and $39,999 by 16.9 percentage points relative to those with incomes below $15,000 (in 1980 dollars). Moreover, they would have to assign a 5-point disadvantage to those who had a parent with a college degree. Surprisingly, they would also have to disfavor applicants from public schools and from urban areas in order to maintain racial balance. (The reason is that many Asian American youth also attend urban public schools.) Finally, they would have to place a negative weight on SAT scores (lower the chance of admission by 4.3 percent for

TABLE 3 *Marginal Effect of Student Characteristics on Admission to Selective Colleges Using Nonracial Criteria to Maintain Racial Diversity*

	Baseline	Race-Blind, Racially Diverse	Race-Blind, Racially Diverse, Equally Selective
Race (Relative to White, Non-Hispanic):			
Black, Non-Hispanic	.154	—	—
Hispanic	.106	—	—
Other Non-Hispanic	−.058	—	—
H_0: Race, Ethnic = 0	.000	1.000	1.000
Family Income (Rel. to < $15,000):			
$15,000–$24,999	−.022	−.048	−.199
$25,000–$39,999	−.028	−.169	−.459
$40,000+	−.038	−.095	−.326
H_0: Fam. Inc. = 0	.762	.000	.000
Parent's Education (Rel. to H.S. Graduate):			
H.S. Dropout	−.051	.028	.229
Some College	−.016	.046	.076
Bachelor's Degree	−.038	−.049	−.224
H_0: Parental Educ. = 0	.427	.003	.000
H.S. Characteristics:			
Urban	−.008	−.115	−.016
Public	−.020	−.144	−.393
% of Class Entering College	−.003	−.124	−.510
H_0: H.S. Charac. = 0	.791	.000	.000
SAT Score (/100)	.026	−.043	.026
H.S. GPA (0–4)	.136	.085	.136

Note: Each estimated with linear probability model. The lines in italics report the p-values of the hypotheses being tested.

every 100 points on the SAT) while placing much less weight on a 1-point difference in high school GPA (8.5 percentage points rather than 13.6).

It is difficult to imagine any admissions committee being willing to put a negative weight on SAT scores. So we try one more experiment, in the third column of Table 3, in an attempt to maintain academic standards. In addition to the constraints of being race-blind and maintaining existing levels of racial diversity, we add the constraint that SAT scores and high school GPA be given the same weight as in the baseline case. Under these rules, we find, admissions committees would have to place even more weight on nonracial factors. For instance, they would have to impose a 46 percentage point penalty on middle-income students relative to low-income students. At the same time, they would have to reduce the likelihood of admission to the children of parents with college degrees by an additional 22 points.

In performing the exercise in Table 3, we also assumed that the pool of applicants at the selective schools remained the same. If, however, the numbers of applicants from private schools, from low-income families, or whose parents had not attended college were to increase, it would likely become even harder for these schools to use nonracial criteria to maintain diversity on campus.

Although an argument may be made for class-based affirmative action in its own right, it is abundantly clear that the substitution of nonracial criteria for racial ones will not significantly cushion the effect on minorities of ending race-sensitive admissions policies. Such a strategy might be more effective in regions where blacks or Hispanics represent a much larger proportion of the population—as they would then represent a larger share of those with various "disadvantaged" traits, leading to higher yields of blacks and Hispanics for any given class-based preference. But for colleges drawing from a national pool of applicants, class-based preferences are not a realistic substitute for race-based policies for producing a racially diverse student body, simply because there are so few blacks and Hispanics with high SAT scores.

Conclusion: Perception and Truth

While the extent of affirmative action seems to be significant at elite schools, there is little evidence of race-based admissions policies at the institutions that enroll 80 percent of four-year college students. Moreover, the suggestion that affirmative action does the intended beneficiaries more harm than good finds little support in these data. Finally, the increasingly popular idea that nonracial criteria could substitute for race-based policies is simply an illusion. In sum, there is an inescapable trade-off between race-blindness and diversity on elite campuses.

The debate over affirmative action is complicated by the fact that the average citizen has little idea of how widely the costs of such policies are shared. Handicapped parking policies offer a useful analogy.[13] Suppose that there is one parking space reserved for disabled drivers in front of a popular restaurant. Eliminating the reserved space would have only a minuscule effect on parking options for non-disabled drivers. But the sight of the open space frustrates those who are desperately looking for a space. Many are likely to believe that they would now be parked if that one space had not been reserved. If so, the sum of the perceived costs is greater than the true cost.

Perceptions of the impact of affirmative action may be similar. At Harvard College, for example, only about one applicant in ten is accepted. Many of the rejected applicants (and, potentially, many more who did not apply) have better grades or higher SAT scores than the minority applicants who are admitted. A large fraction of these may well believe that they would have been accepted if Harvard did not practice affirmative action. Yet only 15 percent of the undergraduate student body is made up of blacks and Hispanics. Even if every one of these students were forced to surrender his place to a white or Asian student (an unlikely scenario, as some minority applicants would certainly be admitted even under color-blind rules), acceptance rates for white and Asian students would increase by only one or two percentage points. If more than one or two percent of those who were originally denied admission believe that they would have been admitted but for affirmative action, then the perceived costs of the policy overstate the true cost.

This example captures quite vividly the conundra faced in the use of race in college admissions. On the one hand, whatever the pedagogical benefits of diversity on college campuses, such diversity may well be under-provided by gun-shy college administrators, since every step of the way, any hoped-for benefits must be weighed against the costs perceived by non-minority parents and alumni—costs that are likely to be overblown. On the other hand, when we approached the point where the pedagogical benefits were close to being equal to the costs being imposed on others, any such benefit was greatly exceeded by the level of resentment produced. Therefore, the misperception of the costs of affirmative action policies is likely to complicate an already complicated debate.

References

Bunzel, J. H. (1988). Affirmative action admissions: How it "works" at UC Berkeley. *Public Interest, Fall,* 111–129.

Constantine, J. (1995, April). The effects of attending historically black colleges and universities on future wages of black students. *Industrial and Labor Relations Review, 48,* 531–546.

Dickens, W., Kane, T. J., & Schultze, C. (in press). *Does* The Bell Curve *ring true?* Washington, DC: The Brookings Institution.

Ehrenberg, R. & Rothstein, D. (1994). Do historically black institutions of higher education confer unique advantages on black students? In R. Ehrenberg (Ed.), *Choices and consequences: Contemporary policy issues in education.* Ithaca, NY: ILR Press.

Herrnstein, R., & Murray, C. (1994). *The bell curve: Intelligence and class structure in American life.* New York: Free Press.

Huber, P. J. (1967). The behavior of maximum likelihood estimates under non-standard conditions. *Proceedings of the Fifth Berkeley Symposium on Mathematical Statistics and Probability, I,* 221–233.

Kahlenberg, R. D. (1996). *The remedy: Class, race, and affirmative action.* New York: Basic Books.

Kane, T. J. (in press). Racial and ethnic preferences in college admissions. In C. Jencks & M. Phillips (Eds.), *The Black-White test score gap.* Washington, DC: The Brookings Institution.

Loury, L. D., & Garman, D. (1995). College selectivity and earnings. *Journal of Labor Economics, 13,* 289–308.

Ramist, L., & Arbeiter, S. (1984). *Profiles, college-bound seniors, 1982.* New York: College Board.

White, H. (1980). A heteroskedasticity-consistent covariance matrix estimator and a direct test for heteroskedasticity. *Econometrica, 48,* 817–830.

Williams, M. L. (1996, November 15). Racial diversity without racial preferences. *Chronicle of Higher Education,* p. A64.

Notes

[1] The author thanks William Dickens, George Akerlof, Christopher Jencks, Chris Avery, William Bowen, Helen Ladd, Gary Orfield, Meredith Phillips, Michael Rothschild, Charles Schultze, Doug Staiger, and David Wise for many helpful comments and discussions.

[2] For students who applied to or attended a four-year college, I added data on the college's undergraduate enrollment, its students' mean SAT score (as reported by the college), and whether it was historically black.

[3] Preliminary analysis of similar data from the high school class of 1992 suggests that this pattern remained largely the same a decade later, except that the extent of affirmative action at the most selective schools may have become even larger. Average SAT scores at the most selective schools have been rising, as the highest scoring students from around the country are increasingly likely to apply to a small set of schools. If these schools have been seeking to maintain minority enrollments while relying more heavily on SAT scores, it is likely that they are doing even more affirmative action.

[4] For a more detailed discussion, see Dickens, Kane, and Schultze (in press).

[5] Those who were neither black, Hispanic, nor white— primarily Asian Americans—seemed to be treated no differently than white non-Hispanic youth.

[6] For a more detailed discussion of these results, see Kane (in press).

[7] The sample is limited to those who reported attending a four-year college. For the GPA results, only the grades from the first four-year college attended were studied. For the B.A. completion and earnings results, if a student attended more than one four-year college, the characteristics of the first four-year college were used. To limit the influence of outliers, those with annual earnings less than $1,000 or greater than $100,000 were excluded from the earnings equation.

[8] For an insightful discussion of the economic importance of these institutions in the careers of their graduates, see Constantine (1995) or Ehrenberg and Rothstein (1994).

[9] This points to another important difference between these results and the Loury-Garman findings: their estimation strategy assumes that B.A. completion has a similar impact on earnings, wherever one attends college. Because they find a weaker relationship between college selectivity and completion rates for black and Hispanic youth, they necessarily find a weaker relationship between college selectivity and earnings for minority youth. Since the earnings results discussed here are not conditional on degree completion, they implicitly include any effects of college quality that operate through completion rates. If Loury and Garman had estimated only the gross relationship between college selectivity and earnings for blacks and whites, even without considering the effects of HBI attendance, they might well have found that the relationship for blacks and Hispanics was the same as for others.

[10] For a summary of the case for class-based preferences, see Kahlenberg (1996).

[11] The results in the first column of Table 3 are not identical to those in Table 1 because the control variables differ slightly and because the statistical technique used to calculate the marginal impact was different.

[12] The second and third columns were calculated under the constraint that the predicted admission rates for all racial groups be the same as in column 1. The third column also assumes that SAT scores and GPA have the same effect on the likelihood of admission as in column 1.

[13] George Akerlof suggested this analogy.

CHAPTER 3

No Alternative:
The Effects of Color-Blind
Admissions in California

JEROME KARABEL

Introduction: The California Experiment

On July 20, 1995, the University of California (UC) became the first major institution of higher education in the United States to eliminate affirmative action. The university's Board of Regents, in banning any consideration of race or ethnicity in college admissions, declared that even the moderate form of affirmative action upheld in the U.S. Supreme Court's 1978 *Bakke* decision—the use of race as a "plus factor" in considering qualified applicants—would no longer be permissible. At the same time, the Regents called for "a UC population that reflects this state's diversity."

The Regents thus placed the university in a difficult position. Since the late 1960s, race-conscious affirmative action has been central to UC's efforts to serve all segments of the population. With the passage of Resolution SP-1, the Regents told the university to devise alternative policies that would maintain diversity within a framework of strict "color-blindness." But data from the first year following the Regents' action make it clear that the new policy will reduce racial diversity on campus sharply.

Both defenders and opponents of affirmative action publicly support racial diversity. Can we not, ask well-intentioned people on both sides of the debate, attain this goal by substituting preferences for the socially and economically disadvantaged for racial and ethnic preferences?[1] After all, the disadvantaged in America are disproportionately black and brown—a point on which liberals and conservatives alike agree. Would not, then, class-conscious policies achieve racial inclusiveness while avoiding the divisiveness of overtly race-based policies?

Many liberals have embraced the idea of class-conscious admissions policies—in part out of a hope to salvage something if affirmative action is eliminated, but also out of a sense that policies emphasizing race and ignoring class are both unfair and politically indefensible. On the other side, UC's conservative Board of Regents (17 of 18 members, all political appointees, are Republicans) included a clause in SP-1 favoring special consideration for applicants who have "suffered disadvantage economically or in terms of their social environment."[2]

Class-conscious policies may be justified on their own terms, but they are not a substitute for race-targeted policies. They will not produce campuses with anything near the levels of racial and ethnic diversity attained by the nation's leading undergraduate institutions and professional schools in recent decades. Racial differences simply are not reducible to class differences, just as class differences are not reducible to racial ones. Indeed, a brief review of California and national data shows that both race and class are important independent sources of disadvantage in the United States today. A failure to grasp this fundamental truth is bad social science, and it will lead to disastrous social policy.

Resolution SP-1, passed by a vote of 14-10-1, prohibited the use of "race, religion, sex, color, ethnicity, or national origin" in the UC admissions process as of January 1, 1997. A similar ban, under Proposition 209, was approved by California voters almost 16 months later. Though a federal court initially enjoined Proposition 209, it did not challenge the Regents' right to implement SP-1.[3] SP-1 provided the framework for admitting students to UC's graduate and professional schools in the fall of 1997; at the undergraduate level, all students matriculating in spring 1998 and beyond will be admitted under the new policy.

The UC experiment provides a kind of laboratory for policymakers and educators interested in the consequences of race-blind admissions. In the two years since the passage of SP-1, the evidence suggests that the new policy is likely to change not only who is admitted, but perhaps also who applies and who chooses to attend. The effect of SP-1 may thus be cumulative, with the new policy having the potential to reduce both the number of minority applicants and the "yield rate" (the percentage of those admitted who actually matriculate), in addition to the admission rate.

The Impact of Race-Blind Admissions on Undergraduate Institutions

Though SP-1 was not in effect for the undergraduate cohorts entering UC in 1996 and 1997, the available evidence suggests that it nevertheless affected the applicant pool: applications from whites and Asian Americans increased by 10.4 and 10.8 percent, respectively, while applications from blacks were down by 7.7 percent and from Latinos down by 5.8 percent (see Table 1). This pattern of change in the racial composition of the applicant pool may well accelerate in 1998, when SP-1 goes into effect for undergraduates.[4]

Though data on the change in racial and ethnic composition of UC's freshman classes are available for only one year (1995 to 1996), a similar pattern emerges: the numbers of blacks, Chicanos, and Latinos declined by 5 to 10 percent, while the number of whites and Asian Americans went up by more than 5 percent.[5] The relevant data for the fall of 1997 are not yet available.

What are the likely consequences for freshman enrollment at UC when SP-l is implemented? Projections carried out by Berkeley and UCLA suggest that the proportion of historically underrepresented minorities on these two campuses is likely to drop substantially—perhaps by one half or more.[6] Other UC campuses, which are less in demand, may well see a smaller drop, and it is possible that a few may witness an increase in minority enrollments, as applicants rejected by Berkeley and UCLA choose to attend other UC institutions.

One other piece of evidence that may be relevant is the case of Filipinos at UC Berkeley. Through 1989, UC-eligible Filipinos received strong preference as part of Berkeley's affirmative action policy; in that year, 227 of them

TABLE 1 *Change in Numbers of Applications to UC from California H.S. Seniors, 1995–1997*

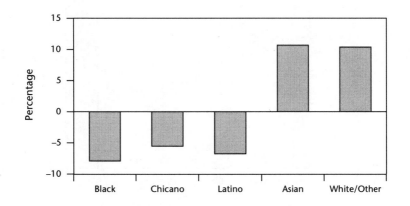

Source: UC Office of the President

matriculated. The following year, Filipinos continued to receive special consideration, but at a substantially reduced level; their numbers dropped to 114, and they remained roughly at this level for the next two years. Then in 1993, affirmative action for Filipinos was eliminated; their numbers plummeted to 54, where they have remained.

The elimination of affirmative action for Filipinos at UC Berkeley thus resulted in their numbers dropping by roughly 75 percent. Filipinos, it should be noted, were much better situated to withstand the withdrawal of special consideration than blacks and Chicanos, whose grades and test scores are considerably lower overall. Though one should be cautious about generalizing from a single case at a single institution, the data on Filipinos suggest that eliminating affirmative action can have a major impact, especially if countervailing measures to preserve diversity are not introduced.

To understand why the end of affirmative action is likely to have major consequences for UC's composition, it is necessary to look at the magnitude of racial and ethnic difference in academic performance. These differences are large, especially at the upper end of the achievement distribution. A 1990 study of public high school graduates in California revealed that eligi-

TABLE 2 *Percent of Public H.S. Graduates Eligible for UC, by Race and Ethnicity, 1990*

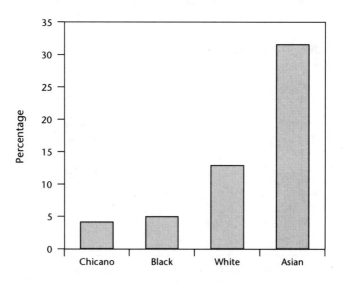

Source: California Postsecondary Education Commission, "Elegibility of California's 1990 High School Graduates for Admission to the State's Public Universities," June 1992, p. 31.

TABLE 3   *High SATs Among California H.S. Seniors by Race, 1996*

	Total	Black	Hispanic	Combined	Combined %
> 700 Verbal	5,442	64	263	327	6.0
> 700 Math	8,130	57	265	322	4.0
> 600 Verbal	25,685	548	1,908	2,456	9.6
> 600 Math	31,786	423	2,062	2,485	7.8

Source: College Entrance Examination Board

bility to attend UC[7]—limited by the 1960 Master Plan to roughly the top 12½ percent of high-school graduates—varied sharply by race and ethnicity, with whites and especially Asian Americans meeting the requirements in far larger proportions than blacks and Chicanos (see Table 2). Of California's rapidly growing population of Mexican Americans, only 1 in 25 high school graduates is eligible to attend UC, compared to approximately 1 in 8 whites and 1 in 3 Asian Americans.

At every stage of the selection process, the proportion of Latinos and blacks who survive grows smaller. Whereas Hispanics and blacks constitute almost half of California's eighth-graders and well over one-third of the state's public high school graduates, they make up barely one-eighth of the students eligible to attend UC.[8] In the group with the highest scores on the math and verbal sections of the SAT—crucial for admission to the most sought-after UC campuses such as Berkeley and UCLA—the proportions are even lower: fewer than 1 in 10 of those scoring over 600 are Hispanic or black (see Table 3). And of those with scores over 700—roughly the top 2 or 3 percent of California's high school graduates—the combined Hispanic-black proportion on the verbal and math SATs is 6 and 4 percent, respectively.

Why Class Can't Substitute for Race

Would taking social class into account in UC admissions, as mandated by the Regents' policy, serve to maintain anything close to existing levels of racial and ethnic diversity? Data on all California seniors who take the SAT provided by the College Entrance Examination Board suggest that a class-conscious policy would have only a limited effect. The reason is that racial and ethnic differences remain large, even controlling for income. Indeed, a careful look at the SAT data reveals that racial differences are actually larger

TABLE 4 *Average California SAT Scores by Race and Parental Income, 1996*

	< $20K	$20K–$40K	$40K–$60K	> $60K
Black	666	737	778	810
Hispanic	711	781	853	904
White	899	933	949	995
Asian	818	925	972	1050

Source: College Entrance Examination Board

among the low-income students who would be the primary targets of a policy emphasizing class. Hispanics from families with incomes below $20,000, for example, average 188 points lower than whites, compared to a 91-point differential for those from families with incomes over $60,000 (see Table 4). These data suggest that the main beneficiaries of a color-blind policy emphasizing class disadvantage would be low-income whites and Asians.[9] Class-based affirmative action is a worthy policy in its own right, but it will do relatively little to maintain racial and ethnic diversity.

The data from California in Table 4 reveal two important truths about the dynamics of race and class in the U.S.: that both are important determinants of life chances, and that they measure distinct dimensions of stratification. National data confirm that race is a powerful predictor of scores on standardized tests such as the SAT, even when one controls for parental education and family income. Conversely, class—as measured by family income and parental education—is an important predictor of performance on the SAT within different racial and ethnic groups.[10] The most disenfranchised students are those who suffer from the disadvantages associated with both class and race. To the extent that class-conscious admissions policies are blind to this reality, they are unlikely to result in racially and ethnically diverse campuses with substantial numbers of poor and working-class blacks and Hispanics.

Outreach Efforts as a Substitute for Affirmative Action

If class-conscious but color-blind admissions policies will not be an effective substitute for race-conscious affirmative action, what about the other proposal most commonly proffered by those who remain committed to diversity and inclusiveness—the broadening of the "pipeline" of qualified minority applicants? While such efforts, which at UC date back at least to the 1960s, should be intensified, the experience of recent decades suggests that the strategy of expanding the pool of UC-eligible blacks and Hispanics is likely to be slow and arduous. It is unlikely that such programs could eliminate the need for admissions policies that take race into account.

UC has been a pioneer in this field, developing innovative programs such as Early Academic Outreach, Mesa, and Puente to improve the K-12 academic preparation of California's minority students. At its July 1997 meeting, the Board of Regents endorsed the recommendation of a 35-member Outreach Task Force, including a proposal to double annual expenditures for outreach from $60 million to $120 million. The objective is to increase the number of UC-eligible black and Hispanic high school graduates from 4,200 to 8,500 over a five-year period. In order to do this, partnerships will be established between UC and 50 "educationally disadvantaged" high schools, as well as 100 middle schools and 300 elementary schools that feed into these high schools. Funding for the new initiative, which has not yet been assured, is to come from a variety of sources, including private foundations and businesses as well as the state and federal governments.[11]

Were the plan to reach its goal, black and Hispanic eligibility rates (at 4 and 5 percent, respectively, in the most recent study) would still lag behind those of whites and especially Asian Americans (see Table 2). Nevertheless, this would constitute a considerable narrowing of the gap, especially within a span of only five years. But critics have already expressed skepticism about the strategy; Regent Richard Russell, a member of the Task Force and the principal author of its minority report, has questioned whether the numbers add up and stated flatly that "the challenges that face us in light of the elimination of affirmative action cannot be addressed by UC outreach efforts alone."[12]

Even if the entire $120 million is forthcoming, UC's effort will be a relatively modest one. More than $33 billion is expended annually for public K-12 education in California, and the system includes over 900 high schools,[13] only 50 of which will be targeted by the outreach plan. If the new outreach initiative is nevertheless successful in rapidly expanding the pool of black and Latino students formally eligible to attend UC, it is far less likely to render these students competitive with white and Asian-American students in the battle for admission to the most prestigious UC campuses such as Berkeley and UCLA. This distinction between students who are "qualified" and those who are "competitive" under conditions of strict color-blindness will be even more pertinent in the competition for places in UC's highly selective medical and law schools.

None of this is meant to suggest that UC is misguided in expanding outreach efforts. But a realistic assessment of the results of efforts to narrow the performance gap between children of different racial and ethnic backgrounds in recent decades shows that progress, while visible, has been painfully slow. The best data source on the matter is the National Assessment of Educational Progress (NAEP), a federally sponsored program that began in the early 1970s and continues today. The evidence reveals that the gap between blacks and Hispanics, on the one hand, and whites, on the other, while smaller than in 1971, remains troublingly large.

Differences in reading skills, though gradually declining, remain substantial. These differences are especially pronounced at the high end of the distribution; thus, whereas 8.7 percent of white students attained scores of 350 or higher—defined as the capacity to "synthesize and learn from specialized reading materials"—only 1.5 and 2.4 percent of black and Hispanic students, respectively, scored at this level. Differences in mathematics were, if anything, more pronounced; 1.5 percent of whites scored 300 or higher, compared to 0.1 percent of blacks and 0.2 percent of Hispanics. As was the case with reading, these differences were nevertheless somewhat smaller than in the earlier NAEP studies.[14]

We should be clear on what these persisting large-scale racial and ethnic differences in academic performance mean. First, they do not mean that it is impossible to have racially diverse and inclusive student bodies in UC's undergraduate or professional schools—a point that has been established conclusively by the vast increases in black and Hispanic enrollments at UC over the past 30 years. Second, they do not mean that UC students from historically underrepresented minorities are in any way "unqualified"—on the contrary, the great majority of them met rigorous entrance requirements and went on to graduate. But these differences do mean that many of them would not have had the opportunity to attend UC or other leading institutions of higher education if race-conscious admissions policies were not in place.

The Impact of Race-Blind Admissions on Medical Schools

The new policy of official color-blindness was implemented for the first time at UC's five medical schools for the class entering in the fall of 1997, and its effects are now known. Applications from historically underrepresented minorities declined 8.9 percent between 1995 and 1996—the year after the Regents' policy was adopted, but *before* it was implemented.[15] This trend accelerated in 1997, leading to an unprecedented two-year drop in applications from blacks (from 1,379 to 1,039—a 25 percent decline) and

Chicanos (from 1,534 to 1,051—a 31 percent decline). White and Asian-American applications also declined during this period, but not nearly to the same extent (see Table 5).

Given the declining numbers of applications from blacks and Chicanos, it is not surprising that the number of acceptances in 1996 dropped as well—from 76 to 62 for blacks, and from 134 to 117 for Chicanos. In 1997, with color-blindness now official policy, the numbers continued to fall: there were only 47 black and 95 Chicano admits. Overall, between 1995 and 1997, the number of black and Chicano admits at UC medical schools declined by 38 and 29 percent, respectively (see Table 6).

Though the final enrollment numbers are not yet in for fall 1997, preliminary figures suggest a substantial two-year drop in the number of minority matriculants. In 1995, 36 blacks and 54 Chicanos enrolled in UC's five medical schools; in 1997, the numbers are expected to be 27 and 39. Combining the two years since the Regents announced the elimination of affirmative action, this constitutes a 25 percent decline in black matriculants and a slightly larger drop among Chicanos.

TABLE 5 *Percent Change in Applications to UC Medical Schools, 1995–1997*

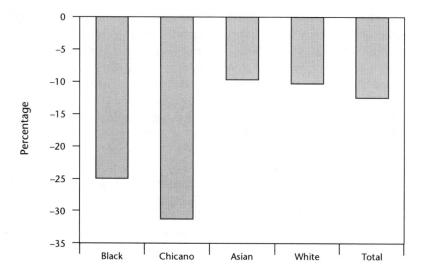

Source: UC Office of the President

TABLE 6   *Percent Change in Admits to UC Medical Schools, 1995–1997*

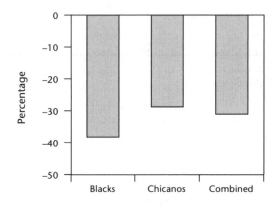

Source: UC Office of the President

A Threat to the Diversity of the Medical Profession

It is striking that affirmative action has been eliminated at the undergraduate institutions that have been most successful in producing minority physicians. Because of SP-1 and the *Hopwood* decision of the Fifth Circuit Court of Appeals, the University of California and the University of Texas (UT) have become the only two major research universities in the country forced to abandon race-conscious policies. These policies have been important not only on their own campuses but also to the diversity of the medical profession nationwide. According to data provided by the Association of American Medical Colleges (AAMC), UC Berkeley, UCLA, and UT Austin are three of the top five undergraduate producers of accepted minority applicants to medical school; both of the other leading producers—Xavier (LA) and Howard—are traditionally black institutions.

Even more remarkably, the UC and UT systems together included 13 of the 18 leading producers of accepted Mexican-American applicants to medical school, with every single one of UC's eight undergraduate institutions being among the leading feeder schools.[16] The elimination of affirmative action at UC and UT thus threatens to narrow drastically the "pipeline" of highly qualified minority students to the nation's medical schools.

What would be the effect on minority enrollments in medical schools nationwide if the entire country were to follow the example of California and Texas in eliminating affirmative action?[17] While a precise estimate is impossible, there can be little doubt that a policy of official color-blindness would lead to a serious downturn in minority enrollments. In 1995–1996, 46,591 students applied to medical school, with 29,236 (63 percent) failing to gain admission to a single institution.[18] While some of the medical students from underrepresented minorities (defined by the AAMC as blacks, Chicanos, mainland Puerto Ricans, and American Indians) admitted under affirmative action would no doubt shift to less selective institutions if race-conscious policies were eliminated, these figures suggest that strict color-blindness would be likely to exclude a substantial portion of them from medical school altogether.[19]

To observe that many of the minority applicants admitted under a policy of race-conscious affirmative action might be rejected under a policy of strict color-blindness is in no way to imply that they are not fully qualified to undertake medical training. On the contrary, available longitudinal evidence suggests that they will successfully complete their training, pass their medical boards, and go on to successful careers as practicing physicians.[20] This evidence contradicts the argument that affirmative action gives minorities an unfair advantage by admitting students who don't "deserve" to be admitted; furthermore, it confirms what common sense tells us about test scores—that they do not necessarily predict who will be a successful student or a good doctor.

Moreover, a careful study published in the *New England Journal of Medicine* demonstrates that minority physicians are far more likely to practice in underserved communities.[21] The end of race-conscious affirmative action, then, would exacerbate the already serious shortage of physicians in the communities that need them most. It is no exaggeration to say that a policy of color-blindness is likely to undermine the capacity of the nation's medical schools to fulfill one of their most fundamental missions: providing medical services to all segments of our diverse population.

The Impact of Color-Blind Admissions on Law Schools

Like medical schools, law schools have often been the subject of key court decisions on affirmative action, with the *Hopwood* decision at the University of Texas being only the most recent example. Under SP-1, UC's law schools, like all other schools and programs within the university, are banned from any consideration of race in admissions. Law schools differ from many other schools and programs within UC, however, in that their admissions policies tend to rely particularly heavily on standardized test scores and grades. Thus we would expect that these law schools would exhibit an especially sharp change in composition as a result of the new policy.

Interestingly, UC's three law schools (Berkeley, Davis, and UCLA)—unlike UC's medical schools—showed no clear pattern of decline between 1995 and 1996 in minority applicants, admits, and matriculants. But in 1997, the first year in which the policy of color-blindness was in effect, minority applications, admissions, and enrollments all dropped sharply. For the three campuses combined, projected black and Chicano matriculants dropped from 43 to 16 and 65 to 33, respectively. Together, black and Chicano matriculants are expected to be well under half of what they were in 1996 (see Table 7).[22]

The most extreme drop occurred at UC's most prestigious law school: Berkeley's Boalt Hall.[23] Between 1996 and 1997, the number of black admits at Boalt plummeted from 75 to 14; of these students, none plans to attend.[24] Among Chicanos, the decline was sharp but not as drastic as among blacks; 27 were admitted (compared to 53 in 1996), and 6 have declared their intention to enroll (compared to 22 in 1996).

While faculty members insist that admissions decisions at Boalt have always been based on many factors other than GPAs and LSATs, a review of the data reveals that even relatively small differences on the LSAT drastically affected chances of admission even when race-conscious affirmative

TABLE 7 *Matriculants to UC Law Schools, 1996–1997*

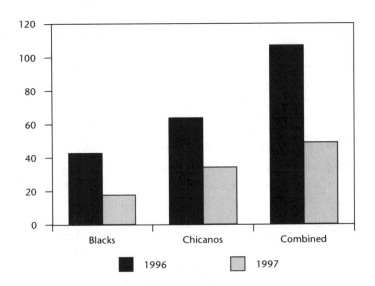

Source: Law School Admissions Offices, University of California, Berkeley, Davis, and Los Angeles

action was still permitted. Thus students with GPAs of 3.75 or above enjoyed an 89 percent admissions rate if their LSAT scores were between 168
and 173; the rate dropped to 45 percent for those with scores between 162
and 167.[25] With affirmative action no longer in place as a counterbalance
to this heavy reliance on standardized tests, the number of minority admits
dropped sharply.[26]

If affirmative action were eliminated nationally and no major reforms
were introduced in the admissions process at leading law schools, results
similar to those seen at Boalt seem likely.[27] Comprehensive data from the
Law School Data Assembly Service, including GPAs and LSAT scores for all
students who took the LSAT in 1995–1996, show conclusively that white
and Asian-American applicants predominate at the top end of the distribution. Of the 3,619 students nationwide who had LSAT scores of 165 or
higher and GPAs of 3.50 or better, only 22 were black and 20 Chicano.
Accordingly, were the nation's top dozen law schools to admit students
purely on the basis of scores and grades, blacks and Chicanos—who together constitute approximately 20 percent of the nation's young people—
would make up barely one percent of the entering class.

Faced with the prospect of a substantial decline in minority enrollments, some critics have begun to rethink long-established admissions
practices. Lani Guinier and her colleagues at the University of Pennsylva-
nia, for example, made a powerful case that the criteria used to admit students to law schools (especially elite ones) have surprisingly little to do with
the factors that predict functional competence as lawyers. They propose a
radical reassessment of what we mean by "merit," as well as a major reduction in reliance on standardized tests. The real consequence of giving heavy
weight to tests such as the LSAT, they argue, is to screen out large numbers
of minority and low-income students who have the capacity to make important contributions to the legal profession.[28]

Taking a similar tack, a group of students at Boalt Hall issued concrete
recommendations on how to preserve diversity in a "post-affirmative
action era."[29] In addition to offering a detailed critique of Boalt's current
policy, the students proposed to increase the weight in the admissions process of such factors as community service and what they call "experiential
diversity."

What Does the Public Want?

Conservative activists and pundits insist that Americans clearly favor an
end to affirmative action, citing the victory of California's Proposition 209
as proof that only a policy of strict color-blindness can express the "will of

the people." But a close examination of the data, including the vote on Proposition 209, reveals a picture of a divided and confused electorate, with no clear majority either favoring or opposing affirmative action.

According to an exit poll carried out by the Voter News Service, the California electorate was sharply divided along racial lines, with well over two-thirds of blacks and Latinos opposing 209. In addition, a clear majority of Asian Americans and Jews—two groups commonly portrayed as victims of "racial preferences"—voted against 209. The passage of Proposition 209 was a result of strong support among white, non-Jewish voters, who compose over 70 percent of the state's electorate despite being slightly less than 50 percent of the population.

Remarkably, more than one voter in four who cast their ballots for Proposition 209 said that they favored affirmative action programs, according to a *Los Angeles Times* exit poll. The results of this poll of more than 2,000 voters strongly suggest that many Californians mistakenly thought a vote for 209 was a vote for affirmative action. Twenty-seven percent of those who voted for 209—well over 1.3 million voters—also voiced support for "affirmative action programs designed to help women and minorities." If even half of these pro-affirmative action Californians voted for 209— dubbed the "California Civil Rights Initiative" by its proponents—out of confusion, their numbers alone would have reversed the outcome.[30]

Americans are ambivalent about "affirmative action." They worry about "quotas" and the admission and promotion of "unqualified" people, but they also recognize that the playing field is not level and that programs are needed to ensure equal opportunities for minorities and women. President Clinton captured this ambivalence well in his "Mend It, Don't End It" speech of July 19, 1995. Done the right way, affirmative action programs remain indispensable, he argued, to the achievement of greater equality of opportunity for all.

In the aftermath of his speech, two national polls examined where voters stood on affirmative action: though worded slightly differently, both found that 60 to 65 percent of voters approved President Clinton's position, with fewer than one in four favoring the outright elimination of affirmative action.[31] Private polls conducted by opponents of Proposition 209 suggested that, had an alternative proposition reflecting the President's "mend it, don't end it" stance been on the ballot in California, it would have passed by a substantial margin.

What are the implications of these findings for those who believe that the elimination of race-conscious policies would do serious harm to both the system of higher education and the larger society? The first—and perhaps most crucial—is that the outcome of the current political struggle over the future of affirmative action is far from settled.

Second, the findings presented here suggest that it may be premature for affirmative action advocates to deploy most of their energies trying to preserve as much diversity and inclusiveness as possible within the framework of strict color-blindness. Instead, their primary task is to make clear that the choice before us is either the continued use of race-conscious policies or the resegregation of U.S. higher education. Voters, legislators, and judges alike must grapple with an unpalatable truth: that there is no easy "third way" that will reconcile color-blindness with racial and ethnic inclusiveness. Ironically, the dramatic victories of affirmative action foes in California have presented advocates of race-conscious policies with an extraordinary opportunity: to show, based on the demonstrable consequences of SP-1 and *Hopwood,* that implementation of the ostensibly neutral principle of color-blindness will in practice mean a return to a level of racial and ethnic segregation in American higher education not seen in more than a quarter of a century.

Notes

[1] See, for example, Richard D. Kahlenberg, *The Remedy: Class, Race, and Affirmative Action* (New York: Basic Books, 1996). For criticisms of Kahlenberg's notion of class-conscious, color-blind affirmative action, see Nathan Glazer, "Race, Not Class," *Wall Street Journal,* April 5, 1995; Abigail Thernstrom, "A Class Backwards Idea: Why Affirmative Action for the Needy Won't Work," *Washington Post,* June 11, 1995; and Paul E. Mirengoff, "Preference to the Poor: Why Class-Based Affirmative Action Is a Bad Idea," *Washington Post,* December 19, 1996.

[2] Minutes of the meeting of the Board of Regents of the University of California, San Francisco, July 20, 1995.

[3] *Coalition for Economic Equity, et al., v. Pete Wilson, et al.,* in the United States District Court for the Northern District of California, Findings of Fact, Conclusions of Law and Order Re Preliminary Injunction, No. C 96-4024 Thelton E. Henderson, p. 35. On April 8, 1997, this decision was reversed by a three-judge panel of the 9th U.S. Circuit Court of Appeals, and on August 26, 1997, the full 9th Circuit panel rejected an appeal by the American Civil Liberties Union (ACLU) to block implementation of Proposition 209. Nevertheless, four appellate judges filed a dissent, and a fifth member of the 9th Circuit concluded that the court should not have upheld the initiative because of Supreme Court precedents. The ACLU has appealed the 9th Circuit Court's decision to the Supreme Court, which will decide the ultimate fate of Proposition 209. See Tim Golden, "Federal Appeals Court Upholds California's Ban on Preferences," *New York Times,* April 9, 1997; Dave Lesher, "U.S. Court Rejects Bid to Delay Prop. 209," *Los Angeles Times,* August 27, 1997; Claire Cooper, "Judges Chide

Peers for Prop. 209 Support," *Sacramento Bee,* August 29, 1997; and Tim Golden, "California's Ban on Preferences Goes into Effect," *New York Times,* August 29, 1997.

[4] In the tables presented in this paper, "Chicano" and "Mexican American" will be used interchangeably. "Hispanic" will be defined as Mexican Americans, Puerto Ricans, and others of Hispanic descent. When figures from the University of California refer to "Latinos," the population includes all Hispanics who are not Chicano. Where available data permit, we will provide separate statistics for Chicanos. Of California's population of 30,895,000 in 1992 (*American Almanac,* p. 34), 8,353,000 (27 percent) were of Hispanic origin. Mexican Americans make up 80 percent of California's Hispanic population; see Census Bureau Releases, 1990 Census Counts on Hispanic Population Groups, CB 91-216, June 12, 1991.

[5] The specific figures for each group are in Jerome Karabel, "The Effects of Color-Blind Admissions: The Case of California and Implications for the Nation," Working Paper, Project on Equal Opportunity, Institute for the Study of Social Change, University of California, Berkeley, August 1997. This paper contains more detailed statistics on trends in UC enrollments and includes a number of tables not published here.

[6] "UC Berkeley's Estimate of the Effects of Regents' Policy SP-1 and Proposition 209," Office of the Chancellor, UC Berkeley, September 6, 1996; "UCLA's Data Simulating the Potential Impacts of SP-1 and Proposition 209," Office of the Chancellor, UCLA, September 16, 1996.

[7] To be eligible to attend UC, students must complete 15 units of high school courses known as the "a-f" requirements (2 years history/social science, 4 years English, 3 years mathematics, 2 years laboratory science, 2 years foreign language, and 2 years college preparatory electives). Only the grades earned in "a-f" subjects in the 10th, 11th, and 12th grades are used to calculate a student's GPA. Students with GPAs below 3.30 but above 2.81 may become eligible by achieving the necessary combined SAT scores on a sliding scale. For example, a student with a 3.10 GPA would need an SAT score of at least 1070 to become UC eligible. For specific requirements and the SAT-GPA formula, see *University of California, Berkeley, General Catalog, 1995–1997,* pp. 33–35.

[8] See James J. Fay, *California Almanac,* (Pacific Data Resources, 1993) p. 36; California Post-Secondary Commission, "Student Profiles, 1996," October 1996 (Commission Report 96-8); California Post-Secondary Commission, "Eligibility of California's 1990 High School Graduates for Admission to the State's Public Universities," June 1992 (Commission Report 92-14), pp. 31–32.

[9] For similar findings, derived from an analysis of a nationally representative sample of high school students, see Thomas J. Kane and William T. Dickens, "Racial and Ethnic Preference in College Admissions," *Brookings Policy Brief* 9 (November 1996). See also Kane's essay, "Misconceptions in the Debate over Affirmative Action in College Admissions," in this volume.

[10] For corroborating data, see Jerome Karabel, *op cit.* Though the data presented here are for whites and blacks only, statistics provided by the College Entrance Examination Board reveal that the same broad patterns hold for other racial and ethnic groups, including Hispanics, Asian Americans, and Native Americans.

[11] See "New Directions for Outreach," Report by the Outreach Task Force for the Board of Regents of the University of California, July 1997.

[12] See Amy Wallace, "UC Regents Panel OKs Minority Outreach Plan," *Los Angeles Times,* July 18, 1997; Stephen Magagnini, "UC Gets Plan to Increase Its Diversity," *Sacramento Bee,* July 3, 1997; and Minority Report of the University of California Outreach Task Force, July 1997.

[13] Data provided by Gerald Hayward of Policy Analysis for California Education (PACE), Sacramento and Berkeley.

[14] L. Scott Miller, *An American Imperative: Accelerating Minority Educational Achievement* (New Haven: Yale University Press, 1995), pp. 45–59. Miller's synthetic volume is perhaps the best single work on the magnitude and sources of racial and ethnic differences in educational achievement.

[15] "UC Medical School Admit and Yield Rates," UC Office of the President, January 15, 1997.

[16] For a list of the 18 schools, see Karabel, *op cit.*

[17] Though the nation has changed in fundamental ways over the past 30 years, some historical perspective may be useful here. In 1963–1964, one year before President Johnson's famous speech at Howard University articulated the case for race-conscious affirmative action, just 2.2 percent of the students at the 83 medical schools in the U.S. were black. Of that 2.2 percent, more than three-fourths were enrolled at the two historically black medical schools—Howard and Meharry. The remaining 81 medical schools enrolled an average of one black student every two years. Thus, almost a decade after the Supreme Court had declared segregated schools unconstitutional, the total black enrollment at medical schools nationwide—Howard and Meharry aside—was approximately 160 students. See Lyndon B. Johnson, "To Fulfill These Rights," in George E. Curry (ed.), *The Affirmative Action Debate* (Reading, Mass.: Addison-Wesley Publishing Co., 1996), pp. 16–24, and "Racial and Ethnic Diversity in U.S. Medical Schools," *New England Journal of Medicine,* vol. 331 (August 18, 1994): pp. 472–476.

[18] Calculated from *Minority Students in Medical Education: Facts and Figures IX,* Association of American Medical Colleges, Winter 1995, pp. 51–57.

[19] Because medical schools admit applicants on the basis of a complex and holistic process (including personal interviews), projections of the impact of eliminating affirmative action on minority enrollments are especially difficult. Nevertheless, academic performance, as conventionally measured by GPAs and MCATs, remains central in determining who is admitted. According to AAMC data for applicants accepted to medical school in 1995, the average GPA of admitted black males and Chicanos was 3.13 and 3.22, respectively, compared to 3.54 and 3.58 for whites and Asian Americans—indirect evidence that race was a significant consideration in admissions decisions. Patterns of performance on the MCATs paralleled GPAs: the mean MCAT in physical sciences for black and Chicana women was 5.7 and 6.7, respectively, compared to 8.6 and 9.0 for white and Asian-American women. An examination of the AAMC data on the MCATs and GPAs reveals racial and ethnic differences of similar magnitude for both men and women; see *Minority Students in Medical Education: Facts and Figures IX,* Association of American Medical Colleges, Winter 1995, p. 58. Combined with the early evidence from the University of California, these figures suggest that color-blind admissions would mean a considerable reduction in the number of blacks and Chicanos in medical school nationwide.

[20] See, for example, *Minority Students in Medical Education: Facts and Figures IX*, Association of American Medical Colleges, Winter 1995, pp. 66–67, 80–81, 84–98.

[21] Miriam Komaromy, M.D., et al., "The Role of Black and Hispanic Physicians in Providing Health Care for Underserved Populations," *New England Journal of Medicine* vol. 334 (1996): pp. 1305–1310. See also Joel C. Cantor, et al., "Physician Service to the Underserved: Implications for Affirmative Action in Medical Education," *Inquiry* vol. 33 (Summer 1996): pp. 167–180.

[22] Since the 1997 systemwide matriculation figures are based on students who plan to register (as opposed to those who actually register), these figures may well underestimate the decline in minority enrollments. In 1996, blacks and Chicanos constituted 108 of 722 matriculants (15.0 percent); in 1997, they comprise 49 of 849 (5.8 percent) of students who say they intend to enroll.

[23] See Peter Applebome, "Minority Law School Enrollment Plunges in California and Texas," *New York Times,* June 28, 1997; Amy Wallace, "UC Law School Class May Have Only 1 Black," *Los Angeles Times,* June 27, 1997. See also Louis Freedberg, "UC Law Schools at Wits' End as Minorities Go Elsewhere," *San Francisco Chronicle,* July 18, 1997.

[24] In 1996, 20 blacks enrolled at Boalt in an entering class of 263. See *1996 Boalt Hall Annual Admissions Report,* pp. 9, 12. One of the three black students admitted to Boalt in 1996 who deferred admission is, however, planning to matriculate.

[25] *1996 Boalt Hall Annual Admissions Report,* p. 21.

[26] Nevertheless, there is still apparently considerable institutional variation in how sharp this drop will be in the absence of affirmative action. UCLA, which placed more emphasis than Boalt on social and economic disadvantage, saw a less drastic— though still large—drop in black and Chicano admissions from 183 to 94.

[27] Concerned about the resegregation at UC and UT, the American Bar Association recently appointed a commission to study the possibility of reducing the role of the LSATs in law school admissions (see Richard Willing, "ABA Plan Would Give Minorities Better Chance to Enter Law School," *USA Today,* August 5, 1997). An important recent study of the projected effects of the elimination of affirmative action on law schools nationwide comes to conclusions similar to those reached in this paper; see Linda F. Wightman, "The Threat to Diversity in Legal Education: An Empirical Analysis of the Consequences of Abandoning Race as a Factor in Law School Admission Decisions," *New York University Law Review* vol. 72, no. 1 (April 1997).

[28] Susan Sturm and Lani Guinier, "The Future of Affirmative Action: Reclaiming the Innovative Ideal," *California Law Review* vol. 84 no. 4 (July 1996); Lani Guinier, et al., *Becoming Gentlemen: Women, Law School, and Institutional Change* (Boston: Beacon Press, 1997); and Lani Guinier, "The Real Bias in Higher Education," *New York Times,* June 24, 1997.

[29] Cecilia V. Estolano et al., "New Directions in Diversity: Charting Law School Admissions Policy in a Post-Affirmative Action Era," Boalt Hall School of Law, University of California, Berkeley, May 9, 1997.

[30] Jerome Karabel and Lawrence Wallack, "Proponents of Prop. 209 Misled California Voters," *Christian Science Monitor,* December 5, 1996.

[31] See Jerome Karabel, "What's Right and What's Wrong with This Anniversary," *Chicago Tribune,* September 24, 1995.

CHAPTER 4

Hopwood in Texas: The Untimely End of Affirmative Action

JORGE CHAPA AND VINCENT A. LAZARO

Introduction: The Lens of History[1]

The Fifth Circuit Court of Appeals decision in *Hopwood v. Texas*,[2] a case filed by four white students who had been denied admission to the University of Texas Law School in 1992, has begun to transform higher education in Texas and has forced the issue of affirmative action to the center of a heated national debate. The case and its aftermath will have both short- and long-term implications for Texas and for the future of affirmative action throughout the nation. Cases modeled on *Hopwood* have already been filed in some other states.

The *Hopwood* court concluded that Texas had fulfilled its obligation to remedy a history of overt discrimination and that it was neither necessary nor permissible to continue racially targeted efforts to raise minority enrollment in the state's public universities. In this paper, we dispute the court's analysis of the current status of educational equity in Texas by reviewing recent cases that sought, for the first time, to minimize the huge historical disparities in public education resources available to the state's minority and nonminority students. The well-documented record of systematic exclusion highlighted in these cases provides ample justification for the continued use of race- and ethnicity-conscious policies at all levels of education in Texas.

Education in the United States has long been regarded as the key to integration and to social, political, and economic mobility. Despite this American ideal of equal educational opportunity, access to public education has historically been limited on the basis of race and ethnicity. This has certainly been true in Texas, where, with only minor exceptions, efforts to improve public education have fallen far short of providing truly equal opportunity. This paper concentrates mainly on the inequalities affecting the state's Mexican-American students.

Inequities in Elementary and Secondary Education

Disparity of opportunity has characterized the elementary and secondary public schools in Texas since the state's inception of an educational system—a pattern repeated with each succeeding generation, including the present. "The history of education," James Coleman wrote, "shows a continual struggle between . . . the desire by members of society to have educational opportunity for all children, and the desire of each family to provide the best education it can afford for its children."[3] While this "desire" certainly accounts for some differences, this same principle—applied even more broadly in Texas—contributed to disparate educational opportunities by justifying even greater inequalities specifically on the basis of race and ethnicity.[4]

Children of Mexican descent, seen both as outsiders and members of a dominated race, were never expected to participate fully in American life. Consequently, as historian Mario T. Garcia writes, Mexican-American children were provided with a "limited education in inferior Mexican schools . . . [that] reproduced a low-skilled work force and kept [them] in a state of economic underdevelopment."[5]

Variations in the quality of education—especially between Mexican-American and Anglo populations—relate directly to local control as the guiding policy for school district governance. These variations suggest a conscious design by policymakers to impose inferior educational opportunities for Mexican Americans and other minorities. Local control, in other words, has served as the apparently rational veil to justify discriminatory practices. "[The] concept of local control," wrote Richard A. Gambitta, "served as a means for political elites, both statewide and locally, to . . . maintain a highly unequal system of educational finance which allowed an adequate education only in those neighborhoods that could afford it."[6]

Jose Cardenas, founder of the Intercultural Development Research Association in San Antonio, believes that inequities resulted from intentional and systematic discrimination. "I don't think that it is accidental or because of ignorance that you have a discriminatory system," said Dr. Cardenas in a 1990 interview. "I think it is intentional, overt discrimination against certain populations in the state of Texas—the minority population, the disadvantaged population, those in low-wealth school districts—that you have a system of school finance which looks after the privileged kids in privileged school districts."

The inequalities in the Texas public school finance system led to a lawsuit that eventually was appealed to the U.S. Supreme Court. At issue in *San Antonio Independent School District v. Rodriguez* was Texas's reliance on the local property tax as the primary source of education revenues, because this resulted in significant differences in per-pupil expenditures. Property-rich school districts were able to raise more tax revenues and thus able to spend more money on the education of each child than property-poor districts. The *Rodriguez* plaintiffs asserted that the public school finance scheme discriminated against suspect classes of schoolchildren (i.e., Mexican Americans, other minorities, and the poor). The plaintiffs also sought to have education recognized as a fundamental right.

The Supreme Court's pivotal 1973 decision in this case, on a 5-4 vote, upheld the validity of the Texas school finance system, effectively ending the attempt to establish a federal constitutional right to education. The Court rejected the plaintiffs' assertions on the grounds that an imperfect correlation existed between property wealth and income wealth in any given school district. According to the Court, any discrimination that did occur was against a diverse and amorphous class that could include wealthy students who resided in property-poor districts. The Court's reasoning in the *Rodriguez* decision laid the groundwork for the difficulties many minorities would eventually face in securing higher educational opportunities at Texas's flagship institutions.

Justice Lewis Powell, who wrote the majority opinion in *Rodriguez*, stopped short of endorsing the state's system of funding public schools:

> We hardly need add that this Court's action today is not to be viewed as placing its judicial imprimatur on the status quo. The need is apparent for reform in tax systems which may well have relied too long and too heavily on the local property tax. And certainly innovative thinking as to public education, its methods, and its funding is necessary to assure both a higher level of quality and greater uniformity of opportunity.[7]

Nevertheless, *Rodriguez* turned back the clock on all efforts to secure equal educational opportunity through finance equity in the federal courts. Because of *Rodriguez*, advocacy groups began to consider the possibility of legal redress through the state courts.[8] Responding to serious concern about the quality of public education at the national level, to successful challenges to public school finance arrangements in other states, and even to the relaxation of doctrines traditionally applied to limit court jurisdiction,[9] these advocacy groups began testing the flexibility of state courts as governmental institutions. The test for Texas began in the early 1980s.

The expenditure gap in Texas public schools was most pronounced in the Edgewood Independent School District (ISD), with its predominately Mexican-American student population. In the 1985–1986 school year, Edgewood spent $2,112 per student on its schools—at the bottom end of a statewide range whose top end was $19,333.[10] The reason for this was simple: a poor property-tax base from which to draw educational revenues. Several organizations—including the Mexican American Legal Defense Fund; Multicultural Education, Training, and Advocacy; and Texas Rural Legal Aid—decided to pursue an action based on state constitutional principles. The result was a unanimous Texas Supreme Court decision that invalidated the state's system for financing public elementary and secondary education.

The Texas Supreme Court based its opinion in *Edgewood* solely on the "efficiency" provision of the state constitution's education clause: "A general diffusion of knowledge being essential to the preservation of the liberties and rights of the people, it shall be the duty of the Legislature of the State to establish and make suitable provision for the support and maintenance of an efficient system of public free schools." This clause, the court asserted, committed the state to a more exacting standard regarding the financing of its public school system than it had practiced in the past. The court concluded that "in mandating 'efficiency,' the constitutional framers and ratifiers did not intend a system with such vast disparities as now exist."[11] The Texas Legislature has dedicated much time to equalizing expenditures in the public schools since 1989, although the improvement from these changes may not be evident for many years to come.

Inequities in Higher Education

Like the elementary and secondary school finance system, the system for funding higher education in Texas came under fire in the years preceding *Hopwood*. At issue was the distribution of state appropriations among the different regions of the state. The Border region received $46 per capita, while the rest of the state received an average of $96 per capita. Ranking highest in receipt of state funds was Central Texas, with $228 per capita. New academic programs that could draw more resources and students were consistently approved outside the Border region in disparate proportions. The fact that the overwhelming majority of the Border region's residents were Hispanic was the basis for a suit, *League of United Latin American Citi-*

zens [LULAC] v. Richards, claiming that the state's distribution of higher education resources was discriminatory.

A state district court ruled in favor of the plaintiffs in 1992, but was reversed by the Texas Supreme Court, which did not find evidence of intentional discrimination. *LULAC* nevertheless had the effect of focusing public attention on the lack of higher education opportunities available to the largely Hispanic residents of the Border region. At the time the suit was filed, for example, there were no doctoral programs available to the residents of this area.

The suit directly resulted in a substantial increase in higher education expenditures in the Border schools, the expansion of graduate programs, and the incorporation of several previously independent universities into the state's major university systems. The Texas A&M International and Kingsville campuses and the University of Texas Brownsville and Pan American campuses were included in the state systems after *LULAC* was filed. The high Hispanic enrollments of these schools reflect the demographic situation that existed prior to the suit. Although the resources available to students at these schools have increased, there are still wide disparities among the institutions of each system.[12]

State-sanctioned discrimination barring African Americans from equal access to public higher education was not at all subtle. Texas had established Prairie View and Texas Southern as segregated Negro colleges. The first African Americans to attend the University of Texas at Austin (UT) were graduate or professional students, because the state did not provide these programs at the black colleges.

Heman Marion Sweatt was the first African-American law student at UT. Sweatt was admitted only after his original application to the law school was rejected because of his race and he filed suit. *Sweatt v. Painter*[13] was ultimately decided in his favor by the U.S. Supreme Court in 1950. The state responded by establishing a "separate but equal" law school at Texas Southern University. Until that facility could be completed, UT responded to Sweatt's admission by starting a makeshift law program for African Americans, in which three professors taught in the basement of a building by the state capitol.[14]

While mandated segregation may have been eliminated from Texas higher education by the mid-1960s, campus segregation has continued to this day. In 1980, the Office for Civil Rights (OCR) of the U.S. Department of Education found that "Texas had failed to eliminate the vestiges of its segregated higher education system and was in violation of Title VI of the Civil Rights Act of 1964, 42 U.S.C. 2000d. . . . In 1983, just eight years before respondents [Hopwood et al.] applied to the Law School, Texas agreed, under threat of federal action, to formulate an acceptable plan to desegregate its higher education system, including the law school."[15] The OCR suggested that, to desegregate Texas's graduate and professional programs, schools "consider each candidate's entire record and . . . admit black and Hispanic students who demonstrate potential for success but who do not necessarily meet all the traditional admission requirements."[16]

At the time *Hopwood* was filed and decided, publicly funded educational opportunities available to minorities were vastly inferior to those offered to white students. Yet the specifics of the *Hopwood* case resulted in a ruling that ignores these great disparities and prevents the use of the most effective means to minimize them. Ironically, one factor that ultimately led to the end of affirmative action in Texas was the law school's flawed implementation of an admission system it adopted under pressure to desegregate.

Hopwood v. State of Texas: **The District Court's Decision**

The appellate court judges who have, so far, had the last word on *Hopwood* ignored the fact that the University of Texas Law School offers an environment hostile not only to minority students but to affirmative action as well. UT Law Professor Lino Graglia made national news in September 1997 with his thoughts on the reasons for minority underrepresentation in higher education:

> [Graglia] said that the only reason UT had given "racial preferences" to minorities was because "blacks and Mexican Americans are not competitive with whites in selective institutions." Asked why, he said that they come from cultures in which "failure is not looked upon in disgrace." . . . [He later said] that he did not see benefits for white schoolchildren mixing with "lower classes" because lower socioeconomic classes "perform less well in school and tend towards greater violent behavior."[17]

Graglia's frequent lectures against affirmative action inspired one of his former students, Steven Smith, to search out white applicants who had been denied admission to the law school. After writing to all such applicants from several years, Smith found four unsuccessful white applicants to the fall 1992 entering class and filed complaints on their behalf challenging the law school's admissions policy as racially discriminatory. The complaints named the state of Texas, the Board of Regents of the Texas State University System, the law school, and a number of individuals in their official capacities as defendants.

The *Hopwood* case was tried before Federal District Court Judge Sam Sparks without a jury between May 16 and 25, 1994. On August 19, 1994, Judge Sparks ruled the law school's affirmative action admissions program unconstitutional, holding that "while certain types of race-conscious admissions are constitutionally justified at the Law School, the 1992 admissions policy under which the plaintiffs were considered and rejected was not 'narrowly tailored' and was therefore unlawful."[18] He identified the separate admissions procedure instituted for minority applicants as the major culprit. The law school had long since abandoned that specific admissions procedure.

The district court ruling was in fact a resounding affirmation of the need for race-conscious policies to mitigate past and recent discrimination in Texas. Judge Sparks's decision was clear and compelling. On the claim of "reverse discrimination," he found that

> [t]he plaintiffs have contended that any preferential treatment to a group based on race violates the Fourteenth Amendment and, therefore, is unconstitutional. However, such a simplistic application of the Fourteenth Amendment would ignore the long history of pervasive racial discrimination in our society that the Fourteenth Amendment was adopted to remedy and the complexities of achieving the societal goal of overcoming the past effects of that discrimination.[19]

On the justification for affirmative action, Sparks wrote:

> The reasoning behind affirmative action is simple—because society has a long history of discriminating against minorities, it is not realistic to assume that the removal of barriers can suddenly make minority individuals equal and able to avail themselves of all opportunities. Therefore, an evaluation of the purpose and necessity of affirmative action in Texas's system of higher education requires an understanding of past discrimination against blacks and Mexican Americans, the minorities receiving preferences in this case, and the types of barriers these minorities have encountered in the educational system. . . . The Court finds, in the context of the law school's admissions process, obtaining the educational benefits that flow from a racially and ethnically diverse student body remains a sufficiently compelling interest to support the use of racial classifications.

Sparks found, however, that the law school's procedure of giving minority applications separate consideration was flawed:

The Court holds that the aspect of the law school's affirmative action program giving minority applicants a "plus" is lawful. But the failure to provide comparative evaluation among all individual applicants in determining which were the best qualified to comprise the class, including appropriate consideration of a "plus" factor, created a procedure in which admission of the best qualified was not assured in 1992. Under the 1992 procedure, the possibility existed that the law school could select a minority, who, even with a "plus" factor, was not as qualified to be a part of the entering class as a nonminority denied admission. Thus, the admission of the minority candidate would be solely on the basis of race or ethnicity and not based on individual comparison and evaluation. This is the aspect of the procedure that is flawed and must be eliminated.

Of the plaintiffs' central claim, that they were not admitted in favor of less qualified minority applicants, Judge Sparks wrote:

What the chart [of Texas Index, or TI, scores] does not prove, however, is that race or ethnic origin was the reason behind the denial of admission to the plaintiffs. Although the plaintiffs had higher TIs than the majority of minority applicants offered admission, the evidence shows that 109 nonminority residents with TIs lower than Hopwood's were offered admission. Sixty-seven nonminority residents with TIs lower than the other three plaintiffs were admitted. . . . Additionally, the Court has reviewed the files of the four plaintiffs as well as the files placed in evidence of other applicants reviewed in the discretionary zone, both minority and nonminority. . . . In fact, of all the applications the Court reviewed, Hopwood's provides the least information about her background and individual qualifications and is the least impressive in appearance, despite her relatively high numbers.

The plaintiffs sought damages. Sparks awarded them one dollar each and the right to reapply to the law school without paying any additional application fees. Not content with this small victory, the plaintiffs appealed the district court's judgment on the merits.

The Fifth Circuit Court of Appeals Decision

Judge Sparks's ruling in August 1994 may be the high-water mark of support for affirmative action in Texas and the United States. Since then the tide has receded rapidly. While *Hopwood* was being appealed, there were several other related decisions with a very different tenor than the district court decision.

In October 1994, the U.S. Fourth Circuit Court of Appeals decided in *Podberesky v. Kirwan* that the University of Maryland's Banneker Scholarship for African Americans was unconstitutional. This program used race as the sole determinant of eligibility. In a further foreshadowing of the eventual fate of *Hopwood*, the U.S. Supreme Court refused to hear arguments in *Podberesky*, thereby letting the Fourth Circuit Court ruling stand. In June 1995 the Supreme Court issued *Adarand Constructors, Inc. v. Pena*, which limited minority preferences in contracting, but was also read by some as limiting federal affirmative action programs.

On March 18, 1996, the Fifth Circuit Court issued a complete and stunning reversal of Judge Sparks's decision. Not only did the court reverse Sparks, it also directly contradicted U.S. Supreme Court Justice Lewis Powell's rationale in the *Bakke* decision that had been the established law of the land on affirmative action for eighteen years.

The circuit court majority opinion opens as follows:

> With the best of intentions, in order to increase the enrollment of certain favored classes of minority students, the University of Texas School of Law ("the law school") discriminates in favor of those applicants by giving substantial racial preferences in its admissions program. The beneficiaries of this system are blacks and Mexican Americans, to the detriment of whites and nonpreferred minorities. The question we decide today in No. 94-50664 is whether the Fourteenth Amendment permits the school to discriminate in this way. We hold that it does not. The law school has presented no compelling justification, under the Fourteenth Amendment or Supreme Court precedent, that allows it to continue to elevate some races over others, even for the wholesome purpose of correcting perceived racial imbalance in the student body.[20]

The core of the appellate decision is that diversity is not and can never be, in itself, a compelling state interest, and thus the law school's admissions process was constitutionally flawed:

> We agree with the plaintiffs that any consideration of race or ethnicity by the law school for the purpose of achieving a diverse student body is not a compelling interest under the Fourteenth Amendment.

Furthermore, the circuit court panel decreed that Justice Powell's statement in *Bakke* that the "attainment of a diverse student body . . . clearly [is] a constitutionally permissible goal for an institution of higher education" no longer applied. Two of the three circuit court judges reread the long-accepted interpretation of this statement and decided that everyone else must have been wrong:

> Justice Powell's view in *Bakke* is not binding precedent on this issue. While he announced the judgment, no other Justice joined in that part of the opinion discussing the diversity rationale.

The circuit court majority supported its radical revisionism with selective references to *Podberesky* and *Adarand*.[21] The bulldozer that the circuit court drove through long-accepted precedent and practice did not change the entire landscape in which admissions decisions could be made. Indeed, it seemed that the court's goal was to change nothing other than completely rooting out any consideration of race from the admissions process:

> While the use of race per se is proscribed, state-supported schools may reasonably consider a host of factors, some of which may have some correlation with race, in making admissions decisions. The federal courts have no warrant to intrude on those executive and legislative judgments unless the distinctions intrude on specific provisions of federal law or the Constitution. A university may properly favor one applicant over another because of his ability to play the cello, make a downfield tackle, or understand chaos theory. An admissions process may also consider an applicant's home state or relationship to school alumni. Law schools specifically may look at things such as unusual or substantial extracurricular activities in college, which may be atypical factors affecting undergraduate grades. Schools may even consider factors such as whether an applicant's parents attended college or the applicant's economic and social background.

The Fifth Circuit Court not only severely proscribed any consideration of race in admissions, it also severely limited the scope of any possible remediation. If a person could indeed show that she had suffered racial discrimination, that individual could receive special consideration at the institution where she had suffered the discrimination:

> No one disputes that Texas has a history of racial discrimination in education. [However,] the *Croson* Court unequivocally restricted the proper scope of the remedial interest to the state actor that had previously discriminated. The district court squarely found that "[i]n recent history, there is no evidence of overt officially sanctioned discrimination at the University of Texas."

As a result, past discrimination in education, other than at the law school itself, cannot be used to justify the present consideration of race in law school admissions. If the Fifth Circuit did not actually kill affirmative action in Texas higher education, it did blind, gag, and shackle it. Seemingly to ensure that no one would ever try to emancipate it, the Fifth Circuit raised the possibility that anyone trying to practice race-conscious affirmative action could be held institutionally and personally liable for actual and punitive damages.

The Fifth Circuit panel rewrote accepted constitutional law to settle the complaints of four applicants regarding an admissions system that had since been discarded. It was not a class action. Several of the applicants had even been offered admission to the law school as it went down the waiting list. The appellate court did reverse the rules under which the plaintiffs could collect damages. Now the law school had the burden of showing that the plaintiffs would not have been admitted if their applications had been considered in a race-neutral system.

The Fifth Circuit's *Hopwood* decision had widespread impact not because of its specific judgment regarding the fate of Cheryl Hopwood and the other plaintiffs, but because it was filled with expansive opinions enforced by the threat of potential punitive damages to anyone who might ignore them. The administrative response at the University of Texas and the Texas A&M systems was to place a freeze on the entire fall 1996 admissions process, then in full swing. The appellate court decision was stayed until the Supreme Court ruled on the issue, permitting Texas colleges and universities to largely complete their admissions decisions under their pre-*Hopwood* rules.

It was widely expected that the U.S. Supreme Court would accept the case if only to address the Fifth Circuit's arrogance in declaring *Bakke* dead. When the Supreme Court denied the petition, the shock was profound and widespread. On July 1, 1996, the ruling became binding precedent in the Fifth Circuit states, Texas, Louisiana, and Mississippi. But what did the law say? That is a matter of interpretation. The possibilities ranged from the most narrow, applying *Hopwood* only at the UT Law School and removing any consideration of race from the admissions process, to the most broad, ordering the elimination of all race-conscious affirmative action programs from all public and private higher education institutions in Texas. The interpreter of law for all Texas public institutions is the attorney general; Dan Morales chose the broad interpretation.

Besides extending *Hopwood* to cover all Texas universities, Morales immediately extended the scope of its dicta to include financial aid, and later to retention and some recruitment programs. While none of these topics was mentioned in *Hopwood*, one consideration that may have compelled the attorney general to take this stance may well have been fear of further lawsuits. The strong language of *Hopwood* and the possibility of punitive damages provided a great incentive for further suits in each of these areas. The guidelines that Morales ultimately promulgated did bury student-oriented affirmative action in Texas higher education.

The Effect of *Hopwood* on Higher Education in Texas

Texas's current and future demography is another important context in which the impact of *Hopwood* must be considered. In 1995, 57 percent of the population was Anglo (white non-Hispanic), but this group composed only 48 percent of the school-age population. All projections show that the Hispanic population will continue to grow rapidly. Under some assumptions, it could become the largest part of the school population within a decade. In spite of increased opportunities resulting from the *Edgewood* and *LULAC* suits, Hispanics' low levels of parental education, high poverty levels, and a number of other factors all work to create barriers to Hispanic educational success. The *Hopwood* decision came precisely at the time that glimmerings of improved minority education first appeared.

The fall 1997 entering class at the University of Texas was the first to be recruited and admitted under *Hopwood*. There was a significant decrease in the total number of freshman applicants from 1996 to 1997, widely attributed to a change in the application procedure. The 1997 application required three short essays; previous applications required none. The essay requirement discouraged the casual applicant.

The proportion of African Americans in the 1997 pool was only 88 percent of the proportion in the 1996 pool (see Table 1). For Hispanics, the 1997 proportion was 90 percent of the 1996 figure. These decreasing proportions may well be due to *Hopwood*. The proportion of African-American and Hispanic applicants admitted in 1997 was significantly less than in 1996. This was likely a direct effect of *Hopwood*.

The total number of applicants to the UT Austin Law School was also less in 1997 than in 1996. The number of law school applications was down nationally, but the fact that the proportion of African American applicants in 1997 dropped by 30 percent from 1996 is certainly a *Hopwood* effect. The most striking effect, however, is that the proportion of Mexican American admittees in 1997 was just 52 percent of the 1996 proportion. For African Americans, the post-*Hopwood* proportion was 19 percent.

The record of UT's graduate programs looks good compared to the law school's. While the number of minority applicants did decrease to 75 percent and 90 percent of 1996 levels for African Americans and Hispanics, respectively, the comparable ratios of proportions admitted are 80 percent and 94 percent. The fact that the share of black and Hispanic applicants decreased more than the share of admittees suggests that there may have been a degree of self-selection among minority applicants. Comparably fewer applied, but more were admitted, suggesting that only the better qualified prospects completed applications.

The graduate business program had a record similar to the law school's. Both programs rely heavily on standardized tests.

Not all law schools in Texas have suffered the same fate as UT Austin's (see Table 2). Most notably, the University of Houston Law School sustained the proportion of admitted African Americans and experienced a 13 percent increase in the ratio of admitted Hispanics. Also striking is the fact that the proportion of admittees of "other" races almost quadrupled and the Anglo proportion of the admitted class decreased.

Several interesting things are occurring here. First, the interim chancellor of the University of Houston (UH) system, William P. Hobby, took a high-profile stand for affirmative action by challenging Dan Morales's interpretation of *Hopwood*. Ultimately, the law remained the same, but his efforts generated much publicity for the UH system. Second, the UH law faculty revised its admissions procedures and minimized the weight given to standardized test scores. Finally, minority students who did not apply or were not admitted to UT Austin may have applied and been admitted to UH.

Texas Southern Law School was created as a response to Sweatt's application to UT Austin. While African Americans are still the largest group of applicants and admittees there, their numbers and proportions decreased after *Hopwood*. The ban on the consideration of race also applies to historically black colleges and universities. Perhaps *Hopwood*-related changes in their admissions procedures account for this change.

The most interesting aspect of data for Texas Tech's law school is the sharp drop in the proportion of admitted African Americans after *Hopwood*. However, the number in 1996, 11, was a very small base.

The figures in Table 2 suggest that *Hopwood* may change the educational pathway of Hispanic lawyers in Texas, but not decrease the number. The combined data for these four major Texas schools show that the Hispanic proportions stayed the same. In contrast, *Hopwood* may indeed decrease the total number of African American lawyers, perhaps by as much as one-third of the current total in Texas.

Far fewer applicants to medical school are ultimately admitted than is true for any of the other programs examined in this paper. The proportion of these applicants stayed about the same before and after *Hopwood*. The

TABLE 1 *Racial and Ethnic Composition of Applicants and Those Admitted to the University of Texas at Austin, 1996–1997*

Undergraduate College

APPLICANTS	1996	1997	% of Total 1996	% of Total 1997	Ratio of 1997% to 1996%
Anglo	10,388	8,843	62.0%	61.0%	0.98
African American	766	583	4.6%	4.0%	0.88
Hispanic	2,418	1,878	14.4%	13.0%	0.90
Asian American	2,291	2,119	13.7%	14.6%	1.07
American Indian	113	59	0.7%	0.4%	0.60
Other	772	1,007	4.6%	7.0%	1.51
Total	16,748	14,489	100.0%	100.0%	1.00

ADMITS					
Anglo	6,854	7,140	65.5%	67.0%	1.02
African American	421	314	4.0%	2.9%	0.73
Hispanic	1,568	1,333	15.0%	12.5%	0.83
Asian American	1,553	1,715	14.8%	16.1%	1.08
American Indian	59	45	0.6%	0.4%	0.75
Other	4	104	0.0%	1.0%	25.53
Total	10,459	10,651	100.0%	100.0%	1.00

Law School

APPLICANTS	1996	1997	% of Total 1996	% of Total 1997	Ratio of 1997% to 1996%
Anglo	2,693	2,511	68.9%	72.1%	1.05
African American	361	225	9.2%	6.5%	0.70
Mexican American	354	306	9.1%	8.8%	0.97
Asian & Other	502	442	12.8%	12.7%	0.99
Total	3,910	3,484	100.0%	100.0%	1.00

ADMITS					
Anglo	841	825	76.1%	83.1%	1.09
African American	65	11	5.9%	1.1%	0.19
Mexican American	70	33	6.3%	3.3%	0.52
Asian & Other	129	124	11.7%	12.5%	1.07
Total	1,105	993	100.0%	100.0%	1.00

TABLE 1   *Racial and Ethnic Composition of Applicants and Those Admitted to the University of Texas at Austin, 1996–1997 (continued)*

Graduate Schools (Excluding Business)

APPLICANTS	1996	1997	% of Total 1996	% of Total 1997	Ratio of 1997% to 1996%
Anglo	6,364	5,555	79.8%	81.4%	1.02
African American	298	191	3.7%	2.8%	0.75
Hispanic	790	612	9.9%	9.0%	0.90
Asian American	482	435	6.0%	6.4%	1.05
American Indian	41	35	0.5%	0.5%	1.00
Total	7,975	6,828	100.0%	100.0%	1.00
ADMITS					
Anglo	2,195	2,305	82.1%	83.8%	1.02
African American	67	55	2.5%	2.0%	0.80
Hispanic	216	210	8.1%	7.6%	0.94
Asian American	184	171	6.9%	6.2%	0.90
American Indian	10	10	0.4%	0.4%	1.00
Total	2,672	2,751	100.0%	100.0%	1.00

Graduate School of Business

APPLICANTS	1996	1997	% of Total 1996	% of Total 1997	Ratio of 1997% to 1996%
Anglo	1,653	1,348	76.2%	77.1%	1.01
African American	102	65	4.7%	3.7%	0.79
Hispanic	174	125	8.0%	7.1%	0.89
Asian American	234	202	10.8%	11.5%	1.07
American Indian	7	9	0.3%	0.5%	1.60
Total	2,170	1,749	100.0%	100.0%	1.00
ADMITS					
Anglo	631	549	71.7%	82.8%	1.15
African American	69	16	7.8%	2.4%	0.31
Hispanic	102	43	11.6%	6.5%	0.56
Asian American	76	50	8.6%	7.5%	0.87
American Indian	2	5	0.2%	0.8%	3.32
Total	880	663	100.0%	100.0%	1.00

TABLE 2 *Racial and Ethnic Composition of Applicants and Those Admitted to Public Law Schools in Texas, 1996–1997*

University of Houston Law School

APPLICANTS	1996	1997	% of Total 1996	% of Total 1997	Ratio of 1997% to 1996%
Anglo	1,628	1,071	62.6%	49.9%	0.80
African American	281	191	10.8%	8.9%	0.82
Hispanic	387	320	14.9%	14.9%	1.00
Other	304	565	11.7%	26.3%	2.25
Total	2,600	2,147	100.0%	100.0%	1.00
ADMITS					
Anglo	678	490	79.5%	57.4%	0.72
African American	32	32	3.8%	3.8%	1.00
Hispanic	79	89	9.3%	10.4%	1.13
Other	64	242	7.5%	28.4%	3.78
Total	853	853	100.0%	100.0%	1.00

Texas Southern University School of Law

APPLICANTS	1996	1997	% of Total 1996	% of Total 1997	Ratio of 1997% to 1996%
Anglo	213	200	18.5%	18.4%	1.00
African American	668	570	57.9%	52.5%	0.91
Hispanic	230	210	19.9%	19.3%	0.97
Other	42	106	3.6%	9.8%	2.68
Total	1,153	1,086	100.0%	100.0%	1.00
ADMITS					
Anglo	67	53	22.3%	18.9%	0.85
African American	161	122	53.7%	43.6%	0.81
Hispanic	66	78	22.0%	27.9%	1.27
Other	6	27	2.0%	9.6%	4.82
Total	300	280	100.0%	100.0%	1.00

TABLE 2   *Racial and Ethnic Composition of Applicants and Those Admitted to Public Law Schools in Texas, 1996–1997 (continued)*

Texas Tech University School of Law

APPLICANTS	1996	1997	% of Total 1996	% of Total 1997	Ratio of 1997% to 1996%
Anglo	982	829	73.1%	72.7%	0.99
African American	44	34	3.3%	3.0%	0.91
Hispanic	230	201	17.1%	17.6%	1.03
Other	87	77	6.5%	6.7%	1.04
Total	1,343	1,141	100.0%	100.0%	1.00
ADMITS					
Anglo	477	442	82.5%	83.6%	1.01
African American	11	4	1.9%	0.8%	0.40
Hispanic	54	52	9.3%	9.8%	1.05
Other	36	31	6.2%	5.9%	0.94
Total	578	529	100.0%	100.0%	1.00

Three Law Schools Above Plus UT Austin

APPLICANTS	1996	1997	% of Total 1996	% of Total 1997	Ratio of 1997% to 1996%
Anglo	5,516	4,611	61.2%	58.7%	0.96
African American	1,354	1,020	15.0%	13.0%	0.86
Hispanic	1,201	1,037	13.3%	13.2%	0.99
Other	935	1,190	10.4%	15.1%	1.46
Total	9,006	7,858	100.0%	100.0%	1.00
ADMITS					
Anglo	2,063	1,810	72.7%	68.2%	0.94
African American	269	169	9.5%	6.4%	0.67
Hispanic	269	252	9.5%	9.5%	1.00
Other	235	424	8.3%	16.0%	1.93
Total	2,836	2,655	100.0%	100.0%	1.00

ratio of African American and Hispanic to white admittees does show significant declines. However, even though the ratio of applicants to admittees overall indicates that medical school admissions are more competitive than law school admissions, it is particular law schools that showed the biggest decrease in the proportion of minorities admitted from one year to the next.

Conclusion

Hopwood has had the expected effect. The fall 1997 entering class at the University of Texas Law School had significantly fewer minority students than before. News of the *Hopwood* case had a chilling effect on potential applicants, and the number of minority applicants decreased. We can expect that a smaller proportion of minority applicants will be admitted wherever grade point averages and, especially, test scores are given great weight in admissions decisions and are used in a formulaic manner. This is the case at many institutions. The University of Texas Law School, for example, gives great weight to the Texas Index, a number that reflects the sum of an applicant's Law School Admissions Test score and GPA multiplied by 10. It is very likely that fewer of the admitted minority students will matriculate. The chilling effect is again likely to be a factor: negative publicity will make Texas institutions less attractive to potential minority applicants from across the country. *Hopwood* will also make it more difficult to make competitive offers of financial support

Most discussion of minority access to higher education has focused on barriers in the admissions process. Finances also pose tremendous obstacles to a more diverse higher education student body in Texas. One of the most troubling consequences of *Hopwood* is that, although the decision arguably represents the law in the three Fifth Circuit states, only Texas has responded by changing its higher education policies. Because of Attorney General Morales's formal opinion, Texas colleges and universities no longer offer targeted or enhanced financial aid packages to minority applicants. Universities in no other state are restricted by this limitation.

Because of the uneven playing field, one of the first effects of *Hopwood* will be a decrease in the overall attendance of top minority high school graduates from Texas at colleges or universities in the state, simply because they can—and probably will—get better offers from institutions in other states.

The obvious remedy for this is increased allocations for scholarships and fellowships for all Texas students. The Texas Legislature could set up its *own* system of scholarships that are portable to any Texas college or university that admits the student. Illinois has a similar program that gives such an award to the top graduates from every high school. Such a system would do much to minimize financial obstacles to higher education and create an incentive for Texas's best minority students to finish their education in Texas.

Legislative action could help equalize opportunity in Texas by instituting a massive overhaul and improvement of elementary and secondary public education. Many of the obstacles to diversity in Texas institutions of higher education begin with differential quality and effectiveness of elementary and secondary education.

Admissions officials could also reconsider the use of standardized tests. A heavy reliance on test scores is sure to decrease the number of admitted minority applicants. If such scores are used, they should not be the sole screening factor.

Tremendous differences in resources, preferences, and policies among the colleges and universities in Texas present obstacles to diversity at each level. There is no simple answer that will provide a comprehensive solution for all the diversity-related problems in Texas higher education. In fact, some of the ideas offered here could have both positive and negative effects on minority students. Without continued careful analysis and monitoring, some of these remedies might end up causing more harm than good.

Notes

[1] The author gratefully acknowledges financial support for this research from the Stephen H. Spurr Fellowship.

[2] 78 F.3d 923 (5th Cir. March 8, 1996) *cert. denied* 116 S.Ct. 2581 (1996).

[3] Foreword to George D. Strayer and Robert M. Haig, *Financing of Education in the State of New York,* New York: MacMillan, 1923.

[4] The term "race" will be used according to the accepted social science interpretation of the word as a social definition or creation. See David Montejano, *Anglos and Mexicans in the Making of Texas, 1836–1986,* Austin: University of Texas Press, 1987, p. 4. According to historian David Montejano, "[Although] race situations generally involve people of color, it is not color that makes a situation a racial one." Id. He continues, saying that "[t]he bonds of culture, language, and common historical experience make the Mexican people of the Southwest a distinct ethnic population. But Mexicans . . . were also a "race" whenever they were subjected to policies of discrimination or control." Id., p. 5.

[5] *Mexican Americans: Leadership, Ideology, and Identity, 1930–1960,* New Haven, CT: Yale University Press, 1989, p. 53. There is much literature supporting this view. Historian Paul S. Taylor was one of the first to report the prevalence of these racist attitudes, in his 1934 book, *An American-Mexican Frontier:* "Mexicans were said to be capable only of manual labor, and in fact farmers were afraid that education would

make them useless even for farm work. As one Texas Anglo put it: 'I am for education and educating my own children, but the Mexicans, like some whites, get some education and then they can't labor. They think it is a disgrace to work. The illiterates make the best farm labor.' "

[6] Richard A. Gambitta et al., "The Politics of Unequal Educational Opportunity," in *The Politics of San Antonio: Community, Progress, & Power*, David R. Johnson et al., eds., Lincoln: University of Nebraska Press, 1983, pp. 133, 146.

[7] *San Antonio Indep. Sch. Dist. V. Rodriguez*, 411 U.S. 1, 37 (1973).

[8] One of the first court cases that challenged the difference in educational expenditures that resulted from differences in taxable wealth among the school districts in a state was *Serrano v. Priest*, 487 P.2d 1241 (1971), decided by the California Supreme Court in 1971. This decision preceded and was subsequently overturned by the U.S. Supreme Court's decision in *Rodriguez*. *Serrano* introduced the principle of fiscal neutrality, which holds that education should not be "a function of the wealth of . . . [a student's] parents and neighbors." See John Coons et al., *Private Wealth and Public Education*, Cambridge: Belknap Press of Harvard University Press, 1970.

Several other state courts have in fact found public school finance systems based on property taxes to be impermissibly inequitable under the provisions of state constitutions.

[9] For example, standing rules and the doctrine of justiciability. See Abram Chayes, "The Role of the Judge in Public Law Litigation," 89 Harv. L. Rev. 1281 (1976).

[10] *Edgewood Indep. Sch. Dist. v. Kirby*, 777 S.W.2d 391 (Tex. 1989).

[11] *Edgewood*, 777 S.W.2d at 396.

[12] Kathy Reeves Bracco, "State Structures for the Governance of Higher Education—Texas Case Study Summary," San Jose: California Higher Education Policy Center, 1997.

[13] 339 U.S. 629 (1950).

[14] Angela McQueen and John Swartz, "Sweatt versus UT," *Utmost*, Winter 1982, 34–38.

[15] Petition for a writ of Certiorari to the U.S. Court of Appeals for the Fifth Circuit, *State of Texas v. Cheryl J. Hopwood, et al.* pp. 8–10.

[16] *Hopwood v. State of Tex.*, 861 F.Supp. 551 (W.D. Tex., 1994).

[17] Mary Ann Roser, "Call to Oust Law Teacher Gets Louder," *Austin American-Statesman*, September 13, 1997, pp. A1, A11.

[18] *Hopwood v. State of Tex.*, 861 F.Supp. 551 (W.D. Tex., 1994).

[19] *Hopwood v. State of Tex.*, 861 F.Supp. 553 (W.D. Tex., 1994).

[20] *Hopwood v. State of Texas*, 78.F3d 932, (5th Cir. March 18, 1996).

[21] In a separate opinion, Judge Wiener, one of the three members of the circuit court panel, wrote, "My decision not to embrace the ratio decidendi of the majority opinion results from three premises: First, if *Bakke* is to be declared dead, the Supreme Court, not a three-judge panel of a circuit court, should make that pronouncement. Second, Justice O'Connor expressly states that *Adarand* is not the death knell of affirmative action—to which I would add, especially not in the framework of achieving diversity in public graduate schools. Third, we have no need to decide the thornier issue of compelling interest, as the narrowly tailored inquiry of strict scrutiny presents a more surgical and—it seems to me—more principled way to decide the case before us." *Hopwood v. State of Texas*, 78.F3d 932, 5 (5th Cir. March 18, 1996).

CHAPTER 5

The *Hopwood* Chill: How the Court Derailed Diversity Efforts at Texas A&M

SUSANNA FINNELL

Introduction: A University in Transition

The most immediate and dramatic effects of the 1996 decision of the Fifth Circuit Court of Appeals in *Hopwood v. Texas*[1] are being felt at two flagship institutions in Texas: Texas A&M University and the University of Texas. One year after the decision, there is unmistakable evidence that the court's ruling has severely undermined these universities' efforts to create diverse, multiracial campuses. These effects are being collectively described by university officials as "the *Hopwood* Chill."

This paper describes events during the first year of the *Hopwood* Chill at Texas A&M, the state's first public institution of higher education.[2] The university comprises ten colleges: agriculture and life sciences, architecture, business administration, education, engineering, geosciences, liberal arts, medicine, science, and veterinary medicine. Texas A&M ranks sixth among U.S. universities in research expenditures and tenth in total value of its endowments. Ranking sixth in endowment value per student among public institutions allows A&M to attract highly qualified applicants.

Thirty years ago, Texas A&M was a small, white, all-male military institution. Much has changed. Texas A&M now has the largest single-campus full-time undergraduate enrollment in the country (34,342 in fall 1996). In 1996, for the first time, women slightly outnumbered men in the freshman class; men, however, still made up 53.6 percent of undergraduates.

A Downturn in Minority Enrollment

Progress in increasing the school's racial and ethnic diversity was slower but nevertheless steady—through 1995, that is (see Table 1). Entering freshman in 1995 included 1,349 students identified as Hispanic, African American, or Asian American, representing about 23 percent of the new class. This number reflected the success of concerted minority recruitment efforts targeted especially at Hispanics and African Americans,[3] who often perceived Texas A&M (because of its history) as neither friendly nor welcoming. Between fall 1991 and fall 1995, the numbers of black and Hispanic students in the entering classes increased by 55 percent (from 184 to 285) and 43 percent (from 622 to 892), respectively.

In the fall of 1996, however, following the *Hopwood* decision, there was a clear downturn in the number of African Americans and Hispanics who enrolled: among blacks a drop of 55 students, or 19 percent; and 178 students, or 20 percent, among Hispanics. At the same time, the number of matriculating whites increased by 529 students, or 12 percent, while the number of Asian Americans went up slightly.

Why this sudden turnaround? *Hopwood* was not yet in effect when the 1996 admissions decisions were made. Similar numbers of minority students were accepted at Texas A&M in 1996 and 1995, yet the number of black and Hispanic students who chose to attend was significantly lower.[4]

Higher education professionals in Texas believe that this drop was an indirect result of the *Hopwood* decision—part of the *Hopwood* Chill. Some students of color and their families, hearing that affirmative action had

TABLE 1   *Texas A&M Freshman Classes by Race/Ethnicity, 1991–1997*

	Asian American	African American	Hispanic	Total Nonwhite	White
1991	256	184	622	1,062	4,947
1992	248	251	644	1,143	4,757
1993	239	237	809	1,285	5,005
1994	214	289	839	1,342	4,608
1995	172	285	892	1,349	4,608
1996	177	230	714	1,121	5,137
1997	224	178	607	1,009	5,015

Source: Office of Admissions and Records, Texas A&M University. Figures omit students in American Indian, International, and Other/Blank categories.

been rescinded, perhaps assumed that A&M would no longer be interested in diversity. Others may have feared that support programs and retention services would no longer be available. Still others may not have understood why universities did not simply defy the court's ruling.

Whatever the causes, the downturn in the numbers is undeniable. With the entering freshman class of fall 1997, the first to be admitted with *Hopwood* fully in effect, Texas A&M was back to pre-1991 enrollment levels for African-American and Hispanic students. Five years of steady progress had been wiped out.

Academic Scholarships and Minorities

Hopwood resulted in the loss of a significant minority scholarship program at Texas A&M, which in turn has had a serious negative effect on the university's ability to attract able students of color. In 1996, before *Hopwood,* A&M's Office of Honors Programs and Academic Scholarships (OHPAS) offered scholarships to 521 African-American and Hispanic students, 269 of whom matriculated at the university that fall. In 1997, with restricted selection criteria in effect, only 288 offers went out to the same pool, resulting in 147 matriculations—a 45 percent drop.

OHPAS, as part of its charge, recruits the most academically promising high school graduates in Texas and across the nation. While the Office of Admission is generally in charge of recruiting, OHPAS targets certain student populations: National Merit, National Achievement, and National Hispanic scholars, as well as the two groups defined as underrepresented by the Texas Higher Education Board: Hispanics and African Americans.

Before the *Hopwood* decision, OHPAS administered two major academic scholarship programs—one for minority students and one for high achievers. The high-end scholarship program was open to students who were ranked in the top 10 percent of their high school classes and also had combined SAT verbal and math scores of at least 1300. Funded by the university's endowment, this program attracted a highly talented group of students and helped place Texas A&M among the top five enrollers of National Merit Scholars in the country.

The minority scholarship program was created in the early 1980s in response to an Office for Civil Rights finding that vestiges of the prior *de jure* segregated system still existed in the Texas university system. It was supported entirely by discretionary university funds. Only African-American and Hispanic applicants meeting regular admissions criteria were eligible for these scholarships. As in the high-end scholarship program, the awarding of these scholarships was highly competitive.

Surveys of students who select Texas A&M show that whites tend to do so because of their sense of the university's traditions. The Corps of Cadets, to which about 5 percent of undergraduates belong, is a small but visible component of the school's military past. It considers itself the keeper of the spirit that surrounds these traditions, which are generally appreciated and respected by the entire student body.

Black and Hispanic students who choose A&M, however, say they do so mainly because of its academic reputation. Thus, sending them information about the university's academic offerings is an effective recruiting tool—as is, of course, the possibility of a scholarship. The offer of an academic scholarship is a potent and meaningful gesture of welcome for students who, for many reasons, still see Texas A&M as unfriendly territory.

A Scramble to Comply with the Law

When the University of Texas Law School (whose actions had given rise to the lawsuit) appealed the Fifth Circuit Court's decision in *Hopwood* to the U.S. Supreme Court in the spring of 1996, Texas A&M administrators assumed that the high court would hear the case—probably in the late spring or early summer of 1997. Thus, there seemed to be no immediate need to revamp the university's programs and procedures. No one seriously considered the possibility that the Supreme Court would let stand a lower court decision directly contradicting its landmark ruling in *Bakke*,[5] which had defined the legal principles underlying affirmative action in college admissions.

But on July 2, 1996, the Supreme Court announced that it would not hear the appeal. Indeed, the Court had nothing to say on the case other than that the University of Texas Law School had changed its practices and therefore the matter was considered moot. Suddenly, *Hopwood*, not *Bakke*, was the law of the land—at least within the Fifth Circuit, including Texas.

Although *Hopwood* does not directly address the use of race as a factor in awarding scholarships and financial aid, legal experts at Texas A&M and most other Texas universities agreed that the ruling prohibited scholarship programs aimed exclusively at minorities.[6] Texas Attorney General Dan Morales, responding to questions from the chancellor of the University of Houston, confirmed this interpretation in an opinion issued on February 5, 1997. Morales further declared that recruitment and retention programs targeted at African-American and Hispanic students would also not stand up to a *Hopwood* analysis.

With *Hopwood* now the law, Texas A&M was forced to immediately rethink all affirmative action policies and practices. I cannot overstate the enormity of this task. The principles of affirmative action had become for us—as for most institutions of higher learning—an integral part of admissions, scholarship, and financial aid decisions.

For OHPAS, the most urgent task was to develop a scholarship program that could withstand a *Hopwood* analysis and to have this program ready for the fall 1996 recruiting cycle. We spent July and most of August designing and getting the necessary approvals for the new program. New application forms, normally available in August, were not ready until September.

The redesigned scholarship program had three tiers, with initial eligibility determined solely by applicants' test scores and class rank, as follows:

Name of Scholarship	SAT Range	Class Rank
PES/Lechner/McFadden	1300–1600	top 10%
Academic Achievement Scholarship	1200–1290	top 15%
President's Achievement Scholarship	1050–1190	top 20%

The first tier corresponded to the previous high-end academic scholarship program, and the funds previously allocated to the minority scholarship program would now be distributed to students in the second and third tiers.

Minority students would compete with all others in the same SAT-range and class-rank category, and scholarships would be awarded on the basis of both objective and subjective criteria. One of the most important factors would be the student's leadership record in school and community, with the emphasis on sustained and progressive achievement; other factors would be awards and recognitions, community service, and employment record (so as not to penalize students whose family circumstances required them to work and thus limited their time for extracurricular activities). The difficulty of the courses the student took in school would be considered in relation to class rank and test scores. Finally, we would read the students' essays.[7]

Data from previous years indicated that most of the African-American and Hispanic students who had won scholarships would have been in the two lower tiers of the newly created categories. To encourage students from underrepresented groups to apply, applications and letters of invitation went out to every African-American senior in Texas with a PSAT selection index of 150 or higher and to every Hispanic senior in the state with an index of 175 or above.[8] Because we expected a larger pool of applicants, requiring a longer time for processing, we moved the application deadline up by a month, to December 9.

The Application Pool Turns White

In spite of the university's efforts, the number of minority applicants dropped by half, while the number of white applicants more than doubled (see Table 2).

Several factors may have contributed to the drop in applications from African-American and Hispanic students. It did not help that the application materials came out late. Moving up the scholarship deadline may have depressed the number of minority applicants as well. High school counselors reported in informal conversations, however, that many students of color had heard that "there were no more scholarships for them," and thought that meant that no scholarships would be awarded to minority students—period. It is also possible that talk of new, tougher requirements scared off potential applicants.

The redesigned scholarship award process was race-neutral. After an applicant's vital statistics were processed, ethnicity (which remained on the application for statistical purposes) was removed before reviewers began their work. Under *Hopwood,* race could not be used as a tipping factor, but other evidence of adversity could—including the socioeconomic standing and the dropout rate of the applicant's high school, as well as the school's performance on the Texas Academic Assessment Skills test. Texas A&M used these three criteria to identify schools—designated Priority One— where students presumably had a harder time succeeding. Students from Priority One schools were given a second look during the review process; those with outstanding academic records could get a plus factor that might tip them into the scholarship offer category.

While there is some correlation between high minority enrollment and Priority One schools, race is not the determining factor. (*Hopwood* makes it very clear that selection criteria that are merely proxies for race are not acceptable.)

TABLE 2 *Scholarship Application Pool, 1996–1997*

	White/ Other	Hispanic	African American	Total	Total Nonwhite
1996	1,744	816	535	3,095	1,351
1997	3,624	524	154	4,302	678
Percent Change	+108%	−36%	−71%	+39%	−50%

TABLE 3   *1997 Scholarship Applications and Offers*

	White/ Other	Hispanic	African American	Total Nonwhite	Grand Total
No. of Applications	3,624	524	154	678	4,302
Percent of Total	84%	12%	4%	16%	100%
No. of Offers	728	206	82	288	1,016
Percent of Total	72%	20%	8%	28%	100%

After the scholarship awards had been mailed, an ethnic breakdown of the awardees (see Table 3) revealed that using the adversity factors noted above had in fact resulted in some increase in awards to underrepresented minorities.[9]

Because the total number of scholarship applicants increased, the overall chance of earning a scholarship decreased. Formerly, white students had a one-in-three chance; in 1997 it was one in four. Overall, the number of scholarships offered to students of color was much lower than in 1996, both because fewer applied and because of the demise of the minority scholarship program. Still, about half of the awards made in the two new categories ended up in the hands of students of color, and they accepted those offers at about the same rate (51 percent) in 1997 as in 1996.

Did our redesign of the scholarship program succeed? Perhaps it can be said that it helped to attract some minority students under restrictive circumstances. In no way, however, was this solution as effective or as efficient as being able to consider race as one factor among many in awarding scholarships. The actual number of scholarship awards to entering students of color in 1997 dropped by 45 percent. At the same time, the administrative costs of the new scholarship program increased substantially: an extra $30,000 was spent on application review alone.

Using evidence of adversity based on the applicant's school as a tipping factor gives some students an advantage; this will include students of all colors. Students chosen under this plan have done well within their educational context, showing determination and perseverance in the face of a difficult high school environment. At the same time, weaknesses in their high schools' academic offerings may cause these students to require remedial programs to help them succeed at the university. Few such programs now exist at Texas A&M, because the university has in the past been able to attract students whose academic credentials predicted success.

It is important to note that, up to now, Texas A&M has been able to retain students of color into the sophomore year (when dropping out is most common) at approximately the same rate as white students: the average retention rates from 1986 to 1994 were 86 percent overall, 80 percent for blacks, and 76 percent for Hispanics. If in the future a disproportionate number of nonwhite students are admitted with poor academic preparation, a racial stereotype of underperforming students will almost certainly be the result.

The most troubling aspect of the post-*Hopwood* scholarship strategy is that the recruiting value of these scholarships is now debased. It will become difficult to recruit and reward with a scholarship the bright, high-achieving black or Hispanic student. Analysis of previous years' awards to minority students shows that many came from middle-class backgrounds and had relatively low need (as do many of the highly recruited and rewarded white students). These students of color rarely came from Priority One schools. Scholarships were what made these students feel welcome at an institution that was perceived as unfriendly towards minorities.

Now this incentive is gone. Unless the student already has a strong desire to attend Texas A&M, it is unlikely that he will pay much attention to the university. Chances are he will be vigorously recruited by out-of-state schools not operating under the restrictive *Hopwood* rules. The resulting brain drain of Texas talent could severely damage a state where minority populations will be the majority within the next ten years.

A Chilling Impact on Recruitment

Scholarships give public universities with competitive admissions a powerful recruiting tool in the intense competition that exists today for academically well-prepared students of color. Robert Berdahl, a former president of the University of Texas, has noted that, although the annual pool of African Americans in Texas who are of college-entrance age comprises 36,000 young people, only 24,000 of those complete high school, only 12,000 continue their education beyond high school, only 6,000 take college entrance tests, and just 1,000 score high enough to meet entrance standards at competitive schools.[10]

Recruitment is a strategic game that universities play, using viewbooks, brochures, letters, and special campus receptions and visits to attract desirable students. The most efficient way for schools to identify promising candidates is to purchase lists of high-scoring students from the Educational Testing Service.[11] ETS maintains a sophisticated database able to configure searches specific to the needs of the college. The PSAT is the source for this database.

To arrive at an appropriately diverse target population, OHPAS might order a search tape including the top 5 percent of students in every ethnic group—about 7,000 names. Previously, these students were invited to a two-day Summer Honors Invitational Program, and about 1,000 would accept. This seemed the fairest way to reach a highly accomplished, diverse group.

In his February 5, 1997 opinion on the application of *Hopwood,* Attorney General Morales ruled out the use of race as a factor in recruitment and retention efforts. This opinion presumably included the use of different PSAT cut-off scores for different ethnic groups. Morales's interpretation created a grave dilemma for our recruitment effort: would we choose a high or low PSAT cut-off?

Using a high cut-off score (195), the number of students of color is quite low—7 percent (see Table 4)—creating a pool that is essentially white. The students of color in this group would be among the most aggressively recruited, likely to be offered very attractive financial aid packages at highly selective schools. Texas A&M is, of course, interested in these students, but in the past has been only modestly successful in attracting them.

If, to reach a larger number of students of color, a much lower cut-off score (150) is used, the total number of students in the mix—more than 31,000, compared with about 4,000—makes the pool unworkable. If we invited that many students to our summer program, between 4,000 and 6,000 would likely accept. Running the program under these conditions would be expensive, a logistical nightmare, and counterproductive to our minority recruitment goals, as white students accept these invitations in disproportionately high numbers.[12] Indeed, it would undermine the very

TABLE 4 *Numbers of Students in Candidate Pool by PSAT Cut-Off Score*

PSAT Cut-Off	White	Mexican American	Black	Total	Total Minority
195	3,694	211	65	3,970	276 (7%)
150	26,793	3,506	1,480	31,779	4,986 (16%)

Source: Estimated figures provided by Educational Testing Service, telephone conversation, April 3, 1997.

meaning of recruitment, as it is members of underrepresented minorities who need courting and convincing; most white students in the pool have no trouble seeing themselves at Texas A&M.

Conclusion: An Educational Imperative

Removing race as a factor in the recruitment, admissions, and financial aid processes at Texas A&M has crippled the university's efforts to increase the historically small number of students of color on campus. Eliminating the scholarship program formerly reserved for Hispanic and African-American students has resulted in significantly fewer students of color receiving awards, at the same time increasing staff workload.

We have found no feasible alternative to working with test agencies to identify candidates for recruitment. If we cannot use different cut-off scores in this effort, students of color will be at a distinct disadvantage. Proportionately fewer students of color take the PSAT, and their scores lie in different ranges from those of white and Asian students. If *Hopwood*'s rules apply to recruitment, it will be very difficult for universities to get their messages into the hands of minorities, and nearly impossible to pinpoint students of color who have excelled.

The *Hopwood* Chill has already wiped out the modest gains made over the years at Texas A&M. Our campus is becoming whiter and less inclusive, a trend sure to provoke anger, misunderstanding, and resentment in the very communities the university has sought so hard to welcome and support.

Simply put, there is no good substitute for the consideration of race in building a college community.[13] Race remains a powerful, distinguishing feature in our society, a feature that is not simply a physical characteristic, but one that shapes a person's experience of learning and of being in the world. Its significance is not comparable to that of one's blood type, as the Fifth Circuit Court asserted in *Hopwood*. Universities must affirm that students of color bring with them a unique perspective that contributes immeasurably to the richness of a healthy campus. This is both an educational and a political imperative.

"Without overstating our successes," wrote Harvard President Neil Rudenstine, "we should recognize that the steady efforts to diversify our colleges and universities have brought about the most inclusive system of higher education ever achieved. American education has grown stronger as a result, and so have the prospects for our heterogeneous democracy. Whatever problems we face as a society, it is difficult to imagine that they would not be far more severe, divisive, and profound if the nation had not made a sustained commitment to opening the doors of higher education to people of all backgrounds, including people from different racial and ethnic groups."[14]

Notes

[1] *Hopwood v. State of Texas,* 861 F. Supp. 551 (W.D. Tex. 1994), *rev'd and remanded,* 78 F. 3d 932 (5th Cir. 1996), *cert. denied,* 116 S. Ct. 2581 (1996).

[2] The author is executive director of the Office of Honors Programs and Academic Scholarships at Texas A&M.

[3] Texas Plan I (1983), Texas Plan II (1988), and Access & Equity 2000 (1993), approved by the U.S. Department of Education Office for Civil Rights to eliminate vestiges of *de jure* segregation in institutions of higher learning in Texas.

[4] In 1996, all non-need scholarship decisions had been made by March 1, just prior to the *Hopwood* ruling; the majority of admissions decisions had also been made by this date.

[5] *Regents of the University of California v. Bakke,* 438 U.S. 265 (1978).

[6] *Hopwood*'s legal precedent was *Podberesky v. Kirwan,* 38 F. 3d 147 (4th Cir. 1994), *cert. denied,* 115 S. Ct. 2001 (1995). This case makes minority scholarship programs illegal, although it does not forbid the use of race as a criterion in the selection of scholarship recipients.

[7] One essay question asked prospective students how they could contribute to Texas A&M's goal of creating a diverse student body: "Texas A&M University is committed to providing a quality education to students who reflect the geographic, socio-economic, and cultural diversity of the state of Texas and beyond. How will your presence on campus assist Texas A&M in realizing this goal?" A second, optional essay invited students to write about any personal situation, exceptional hardship, temporary failure, or other experience that had shaped their goals.

[8] The selection index is derived by doubling the verbal score and adding the math score on the PSAT, which students take in October of the junior year of high school.

[9] This confirms the findings of an extensive report completed for the Texas Higher Education Coordinating Board by the Advisory Committee on Criteria for Diversity, *Alternative Diversity Criteria: Analyses and Recommendations,* in January 1997: "It must be recognized that no single [criterion] or combination of criteria examined results in the same level of minority participation as occurred under criteria used prior to *Hopwood.* The additive use of multiple criteria merits consideration. Using criteria of income (or poverty) and parents' level of education [produced] relatively large eligible underserved populations which include more than 50 percent minority group members."

[10] *New York Times,* March 13, 1997, p. C24.

[11] Personal contacts with high school counselors are useful, but it is unrealistic to rely on them to contact every minority student who might be interested in Texas

A&M because of the large number of schools. In 1996, half of all the black students entering the university were the only African American representative of their high school in the freshman class. Only seven high schools sent more than five black students each. A similar pattern held for Hispanics: 201 high schools sent just one Hispanic student to Texas A&M; 34 schools sent more than five students per school.

[12] This was confirmed by the college preview program Admit One, which had existed for years. Prior to *Hopwood,* Admit One invited black and Hispanic students who had been admitted to Texas A&M to come for a one-day welcome to the university with a preview of academic support services, multicultural programs, mentoring services for minority students, and the like. *Hopwood* made such a program illegal. Instead, admitted students from Priority One schools were invited to Admit One in 1997. The majority of students who accepted were white, even though the invitation said that the day was meant to highlight programs aimed at minorities.

[13] See Advisory Committee, *Alternative Diversity Criteria.*

[14] *Chronicle of Higher Education,* April 19, 1996, p. B1.

CHAPTER 6

Notes from the Field: Higher Education Desegregation in Mississippi

ROBERT A. KRONLEY AND CLAIRE V. HANDLEY

Introduction

The U.S. Supreme Court ruled in 1992, in *United States v. Fordice,* that states which had previously operated legally segregated systems of higher education must take affirmative steps to rid themselves of the remnants of segregation in their colleges and universities.[1] The Court directed that these efforts take place pursuant to "sound educational practices."[2] The mandate to desegregate public higher education—and to give weight to the experience and opinions of educators in crafting effective remedies—held out the possibility of infusing opportunity into systems in which blacks' access to and success in college had lagged.[3]

This paper reviews the steps Mississippi, the state from which the *Fordice* litigation arose, has taken to desegregate its public system of higher education in the five years since the Supreme Court's decision. During this time, litigation in *Fordice* has continued, and the state has proposed and revised—sometimes under court order—a number of remedies. Some of these proposals have gained wide acceptance; others are controversial.

While it is too early to make conclusive judgments about either the effectiveness or the ultimate fairness of Mississippi's actions, a look at the recent desegregation process in the state provides insight into concerns shared by all nineteen states affected by the *Fordice* decision. These concerns include black student representation in higher education, the future of historically black colleges and universities, the use of race-based financial aid, and the need for systemic solutions to continuing educational problems that arise out of a history of inequitable and segregative policies and practices.

United States v. Fordice

Higher education desegregation in Mississippi began in 1975 when a group of black citizens went into federal court to ask that the state provide a desegregated and more equitable system. Years of negotiation and attempts at settlement followed the initial filing of the lawsuit. During this period, the Board of Trustees of the state's Institutions of Higher Learning (IHL), the governing body of Mississippi's eight four-year public universities, adopted nonracial mission statements for each university. While each institution later issued admission policies that no longer explicitly excluded students on the basis of race, enrollment at the traditionally white campuses remained largely white and those at the three historically black universities continued to be overwhelmingly black.

Attempts at voluntary resolution proved fruitless and, in 1987, the case went to trial. The district court held that Mississippi's legal duty to desegregate its universities extended only to ensuring that its policies were racially neutral, developed and implemented in good faith, and did not contribute substantially to the racial identifiability of individual schools. Applying this analysis, the district court concluded that Mississippi was not violating federal law and that no remedies were required.[4] The U.S. Court of Appeals for the Fifth Circuit affirmed the ruling.[5]

The federal government joined the plaintiffs, and the Supreme Court agreed to hear an appeal from the Fifth Circuit decision. On June 26, 1992, the Court ruled that Mississippi's adoption of race-neutral policies in public higher education was not enough to dismantle fully the former *de jure* segregated system. The Court held that "if policies traceable to the *de jure* system are still in force and having discriminatory effects, those policies too must be reformed to the extent practical and consistent with sound educational practice."

The Court ruled that, even though a state may abandon a racially segregative policy, there might still be state action arising out of previous policies that fosters continued segregation. Mississippi, the Court found, maintained policies and practices traceable to the *de jure* segregated system that continued to have discriminatory effects substantially restricting individuals' choice of institution and contributing to the racial identifiability of those institutions. The Court named four such remnants—admission standards, program duplication, institutional mission assignments, and the continuing operation of eight separate public universities—and explicitly noted the possibility of other suspect policies and practices in Mississippi.[6]

Fordice said that the adoption of race-neutral policies alone might not be a sufficient remedy in the nineteen states that had previously operated legally segregated systems of higher education. It held that vestiges of segregation must be eradicated from those systems, and charged the states with an affirmative duty to do so. Finally, *Fordice* indicated that lower courts should defer to some degree to educators in crafting appropriate desegregation remedies. The Supreme Court remanded the case to the district court to determine whether Mississippi had met its obligation to dismantle the prior dual system.

Mississippi's Response

After the Supreme Court's ruling and prior to the district court hearing, the IHL Board proposed a limited reorganization of the state's system of higher education, including new systemwide admission standards that would replace a multi-tiered system based entirely on ACT scores. Under the old system, students could be admitted to the state's historically black universities with lower ACT scores than were required of applicants to the traditionally white universities. The proposed new standards required higher scores for admission to historically black universities.

Under the new standards, students would be admitted to any of Mississippi's public universities if they met one of the following requirements:

1. A high school grade point average (GPA) of at least 3.2 in a college preparatory (core) curriculum;
2. A GPA under 3.2 but equal to or greater than 2.5 in the core curriculum, *or* a ranking in the top 50 percent of the high school graduating class *and* a minimum ACT score of 16; or
3. A GPA of 2.0 or higher *and* an ACT score of 18 or higher.

Also, student athletes who were "full qualifiers" under the NCAA Division 1 guidelines effective August 1, 1996, would be automatically admitted.

Students who did not qualify for full admission could be admitted conditionally. Some of these students would be required to participate in a summer developmental program; those who successfully completed the program would be admitted to the university and offered a new year-long academic support program. Students who failed to complete the summer program would be advised of other options and assisted in pursuing them.

In doing away with the differential admission standards among its universities, the state also abolished remedial programs at these institutions. As a result, universities could no longer provide targeted classes to entering students who had not received adequate preparation in the state's elementary and secondary schools.

Proponents of the new admission requirements saw them as an effective and immediate means to rid the state of one of the vestiges of segregation identified by the Supreme Court. They also argued that the adoption of more rigorous standards for all students aligned the state's public universities with national and regional trends.

The new standards, however, generated great concern about access to higher education for black students. Critics questioned whether many of the state's public high schools really prepared students to meet the new standards. They emphasized that—unlike other states—Mississippi had no plan for systemic cooperation between the higher education system and elementary and secondary education, and they questioned the fairness of implementing the new standards immediately. Georgia and Maryland, for example, had each determined to phase in new, more rigorous college admission standards over several years. During the phase-in, the higher education systems in these states would undertake comprehensive efforts to improve K-12 education and align institutional expectations with preparatory approaches that help students meet those expectations.

Some analysts also saw Mississippi's reliance on two-year colleges to prepare unqualified students for admission to four-year institutions as overly optimistic. Two-year colleges in Mississippi had not proved an effective route to the bachelor's degree, particularly for black students, and the proposed plan included no strategy to help them become effective.

Furthermore, Mississippi's proposed standards also had the potential to penalize less well-off students—blacks prominent among them. The summer developmental program for students who did not automatically qualify for full admission would, in 1996, cost participants from $1,931 to $2,927, depending on the institution in which they enrolled. Students who qualified for Pell grants would still need to come up with at least $761 to take part in the program—not to mention sacrificing summer earnings. For low-income students, therefore, the cost of attending the summer session might be prohibitive.

The Board's reorganization proposal also included plans to reduce the number of universities from eight to six by incorporating the Mississippi University for Women into Mississippi State University, and by consolidating historically black Mississippi Valley State University and nearby traditionally white Delta State University into a new Delta Valley State

University, situated on the campus of Delta State. In addition, the Board proposed program enhancements for the state's two other historically black universities, Alcorn State and Jackson State.

The District Court's Order and the State's Response

On March 10, 1995, the district court issued a Memorandum Opinion and Remedial Decree in the case, now known as *Ayers v. Fordice.*[7] Among other actions, the court

- Approved the new systemwide uniform admission standards developed by the IHL Board, observing that "while the new admission standards may reduce the number of black students eligible to be admitted to the system without remedial courses required, it is not evident that the new standards will actually reduce the number of black students ultimately admitted to the system as either regular or remediated admittees."
- Ordered program and financial enhancements at Alcorn State and Jackson State. Program enhancements included creation of non-duplicative programs in allied health, social work (Ph.D.), and urban planning (M.A./Ph.D.) at Jackson State and an MBA program and a small-farm development center at Alcorn State. Financial enhancements included funds to improve facilities at Jackson State and the creation of two trusts of $5 million each for Jackson State and Alcorn State. The court ordered that the income from these trusts be used for continuing educational enhancement and racial diversity. The court specifically directed the state to consider the use of other-race scholarships for white applicants to these institutions.
- Refused to order the incorporation of Mississippi University for Women into Mississippi State University.
- Deferred the consolidation of Mississippi Valley State and Delta State pending the findings of a study commissioned by the IHL Board (see below).
- Ordered the IHL Board to undertake studies of

    1. the feasibility of establishing systemwide coordination between universities and community colleges in the areas of admission standards and articulation agreements (the community college study);
    2. the relative strengths and weaknesses of existing programs at Jackson State to determine how the institution might best achieve the

urban emphasis of its mission, and to evaluate the feasibility and educational soundness of establishing an engineering school, a law school, and a five-year pharmacy program (the Jackson State study);

3. the practicability of the IHL Board assuming control of facility maintenance funds at each of the eight universities (the facilities maintenance study); and

4. any educationally sound alternatives to the proposed merger of Mississippi Valley State University with its neighbor, Delta State University (the Delta study).

- Ordered the establishment of a three-person monitoring committee to oversee implementation of the decree.

The *Fordice* plaintiffs, while pleased with some of the proposed enhancements to the historically black colleges, were distressed at the court's finding regarding the new admission standards and at other elements of the court's decree. They appealed the decision.

Initial progress in implementing the various elements of the district court's 1995 order has been uneven. The monitoring committee, whose members were to have been agreed upon by all the parties by May 1, 1995, or, in the absence of such agreement, appointed by the court, has not been named. The court has since informed the parties that it no longer intends to ratify or appoint the members of the monitoring committee until appeals in the matter are completed.

The Board commissioned three of the four studies ordered by the court: on facilities maintenance, on Jackson State, and on the Delta State merger. It did not proceed with the study on the relationship between the university system and the state's community colleges. Rather, IHL staff and community college system leaders are discussing the possibility of greater systemic cooperation between them.

Of the three commissioned reports, the Delta study and the Jackson State study have particular importance for minority students and for the future of historically black institutions in the state. The Delta study was submitted to the Board in March 1996. It found that desegregated high-quality higher education in the Mississippi Delta is not contingent on consolidation of Mississippi Valley State and Delta State. Its authors made ten recommendations that they considered less drastic and more practicable and educationally sound than consolidation. The recommendations included:

- Tangible commitments from the Board to a desegregated system of public higher education that embraces opportunity.

- A revised mission statement for Mississippi Valley State.
- Shared programs and closer cooperation between the Delta's universities and community colleges. These included institutes for effective teaching practices and for Delta culture and community, each to be operated jointly by Delta State and Mississippi Valley State.
- Systemic involvement by institutions of higher learning with public schools.
- The creation of new programs at Mississippi Valley State, including recording industry management, special education, history, and public policy.
- The use of other-race scholarships at both universities.
- Increased funding tied to specific accountability for both universities.[8]

Following submission of the study, the Board formally decided not to merge Delta State and Mississippi Valley State. It deferred consideration of the other recommendations.

The Jackson State study was submitted to the Board in November 1996. Its 30 recommendations included

- Development of new schools of engineering and of allied health.
- Increased investment in teacher preparation.
- Concerted efforts to strengthen recruitment and retention.
- Significant improvements to the physical plant.
- Strengthened relations with the surrounding community.[9]

The report did not recommend the creation of a new law school at Jackson State University, nor did it recommend moving existing programs at other institutions to Jackson State. The Board has not yet acted on the Jackson State study.

Both the Delta and the Jackson State studies recommended significant program enhancements for historically black universities. These enhancements were viewed as a means to increase and strengthen each institution's academic offerings and to attract white students. Administrators at the affected schools responded favorably to these recommendations. Initial responses to both studies by faculty and administrators at other universities (Delta State University and the University of Mississippi most prominently) have been generally supportive of the recommendations.

Enhancement of the historically black universities also garnered legislative support. In response to the district court's order and a subsequent recommendation by the Board, the legislature set aside $15 million for an *Ayers* endowment trust. Interest and income from the trust is to be distributed equally among the three historically black institutions; these funds are to be used to promote desegregation through compliance with the district court's order. In addition to program enhancement, use of race-specific scholarships to recruit white students is expressly contemplated.

Initial Impact: Black Enrollment Declines

Despite continuing protests and the appeal to the Fifth Circuit Court, the new admission standards were implemented in time for the 1996–1997 school year. The apparent result was a significant decline in black enrollment in Mississippi's public universities.

Between fall 1995 and fall 1996, first-time full-time black freshmen enrollment at Mississippi's eight public universities fell by 463 students (see Table 1). The representation of blacks among freshmen fell from 43 percent to 38 percent. Most of the decline was at the three historically black universities: the number of black freshmen dropped 12 percent at Alcorn State, 24 percent at Jackson State, and 27 percent at Mississippi Valley State. Two institutions, the University of Mississippi and Delta State University, saw an increase in both the number and percentage of black freshmen. These increases, however, were slight in comparison to the overall decline in black freshmen throughout the system.

It is possible that some of this decline can be attributed to normal year-to-year fluctuations. But the representation of blacks among first-time

TABLE 1   *First-Time Full-Time Black Freshmen Enrollment: 1995–1996*

	1995	*1996*	*Difference '95 to '96*	*Percent Change*
Alcorn State University	693	613	−80	−12%
Delta State University	120	135	15	+13%
Jackson State University	1,091	834	−257	−24%
Mississippi State University	319	265	−54	−17%
Mississippi U. for Women	65	58	−7	−11%
Mississippi Valley State U.	440	321	−119	−27%
University of Mississippi	126	170	44	+35%
U. of Southern Mississippi	359	354	−5	−1%
System Total	3,213	2,750	−463	−14%
Percent of all freshmen	43%	38%		

Source: Mississippi Institutions of Higher Learning, Office of Policy and Budget

TABLE 2   *Summer Developmental Program, 1996–1997 Comparison*

	1996	1997	Difference '96 to '97	Percent Change
Alcorn State University	60	50	-10	–17%
Delta State University	0	8	+8	—
Jackson State University	47	103	+56	+119%
Mississippi State University	9	18	+9	+100%
Mississippi U. for Women	6	9	+3	+50%
Mississippi Valley State U.	76	82	+6	+8%
University of Mississippi	1	8	+7	+700%
U. of Southern Mississippi	5	17	+12	+240%
System Total	204	295	+91	+45%

Source: Mississippi Institutions of Higher Learning, Office of Planning and Budget

full-time freshmen had been relatively stable during the 1990s, and it is unlikely that routine variations can account for the scope of the decrease.

Furthermore, with this decline, Mississippi now has fewer black freshmen and lower representation of them in the cohort than it did twenty years ago. In 1976 there were 3,506 black freshmen enrolled in Mississippi's eight public universities, representing 40.5 percent of all freshmen.[10] In 1996, as we see above, there were 756 fewer black students, and their representation had declined to 38 percent.

The significant decline between 1995 and 1996 in black freshmen enrollment may have resulted in part from inadequate communication about the summer program. During the program's first year, 204 blacks enrolled; 188 were admitted to the system's institutions the following fall (see Table 2).[11] In 1997, following heightened efforts to reach black students and their families, 295 blacks participated in the summer program. Data are not yet available on how many successfully completed the program and enrolled at a Mississippi university in the fall. While the increase in summer program participation is a hopeful sign, it still leaves far fewer black freshmen likely to enroll in fall 1997 than in fall 1995.

While Mississippi has adopted policies designed to remove race as a factor in admission decisions, it has committed itself to considering race in financial aid policies as a means to desegregate its universities. This practice was encouraged by the district court's order, which specifically contemplates race-based scholarships for white students at historically black institutions. In March 1996, Mississippi's use of race-sensitive means to desegregate its institutions appeared to be threatened by the decision of the U.S. Court of Appeals for the Fifth Circuit in *Hopwood v. University of Texas School of Law*.[12] *Hopwood* overturned the law school's race-sensitive admission and financial aid policies, which had been designed in part to desegregate the institution. In so doing, *Hopwood* also rejected the prevailing rationale that the goal of promoting student diversity allows institutions to consider race in the admissions process.

Although Mississippi is in the Fifth Circuit, reaction to *Hopwood* in the state has been muted. In October 1996, the IHL Board filed a motion with the district court asking for "direction to continue affirmative other-race faculty and staff employment and student enrollment practices," at least until after the appeal on admission standards was heard. The United States filed a similar motion. The district court has not yet responded to these motions, and race-sensitive policies in Mississippi's universities have been left undisturbed.

Fordice and the Fifth Circuit

In April 1997, the Fifth Circuit Court upheld the district court's 1995 approval of the new admission standards.[13] In doing so, it agreed with the district court's conclusion that the proposed spring assessment and summer remedial programs would alleviate the "disproportionate impact" of the new standards on black students who are "capable, with remedial education," of doing college-level work. The court characterized arguments in favor of lower admission standards to ensure greater black representation as "educationally unsound," because some of the students admitted under lower admission standards would not be prepared to do college level work.

While upholding the admission standards, however, the appeals court recommended that the district court monitor the spring assessment and summer remedial programs' effectiveness in identifying and admitting students capable of doing college-level work after appropriate remediation.[14] The court also questioned the soundness of eliminating remedial courses offered during the academic year on university campuses and asked the district court to contemplate their reinstatement.

The appeals court's concern about the efficacy of the spring assessment and summer remedial programs in the absence of remediation during the academic year recognizes, at least tacitly, that equitable access to higher education depends in large degree on effective preparation in elementary and secondary education. While the court's decision does not approach, or even consider, comprehensive remedies that effectively link what happens in K-12 education to college admissions, its directive to the district court to look closely at aspects of the admissions process suggests that the state may wish to revisit how the new admission standards are being implemented if there is no improvement in minority access to public higher education in the state.

The Fifth Circuit Court's ruling also affects the state's historically black universities. It ordered a new study of the feasibility of additional academic and land-grant programs to desegregate Alcorn State University. It also requested clarification of the status of the Board's proposal to merge Mississippi Valley State and Delta State and ordered the district court to determine the status of efforts to accredit business programs at Jackson State. With the exception of the new study ordered for Alcorn State, the investigations of historically black universities have already been completed, and it is the Board's intention to act on these studies' recommendations and submit its decisions to the district court.

Furthermore, the appeals court reversed the district court's finding that Mississippi's use of ACT cut-off scores in allocating undergraduate scholarships was permissible. The court ruled that such reliance on ACT scores resulted in the disproportionate award of scholarships to white students even though black students were more likely to need financial aid. The appeals court remanded this issue for determination of whether an educationally sound and practicable remedy could be implemented. In its discussion of scholarships, the court noted that Mississippi's traditionally white institutions "offered some scholarships specifically for black applicants." In recognizing the "availability of a small number of minority scholarships at historically white institutions," the court made no reference to its previous decision in *Hopwood*, which limited the use of these measures when they are not narrowly tailored to remedy past discrimination. Mississippi's racially targeted scholarships, imposed pursuant to a court order, thus appear to be unaffected by *Hopwood*.

Conclusion

New admission requirements, increased commitment to race-sensitive policies, and proposed enhancements at the historically black colleges and universities are the most tangible outcomes thus far of 22 years of litigation in *United States v. Fordice*. Events in Mississippi are still unfolding, and it is premature to posit a series of lessons from Mississippi's experience, or to draw authoritative conclusions about it. There are, however, some observations that will enable us to help chart Mississippi's progress over the next few years.

The April 1997 Fifth Circuit Court ruling in *Fordice* seems likely to end the dominant role that litigation has played in higher education in Mississippi since 1975. Both the plaintiffs and the state initially expressed interest in ending the lawsuit and undertook settlement negotiations. Although the meetings did not produce an agreement and the plaintiffs intend to seek a Supreme Court review of the case, both sides continue to express a preference for settlement.[15] Moreover, it is doubtful that any further appeals will result in significant changes to the appeals court's decision. *Hopwood* has had almost no immediate impact on higher education policy in the state; there is, at this writing, no discernible effort in Mississippi to bring a *Hopwood*-based suit challenging the IHL Board's race-sensitive policies.

As a result, educators and other public officials will regain substantial autonomy, along with the responsibility and authority to develop and implement policies to continue to desegregate the system. Desegregation, however, is a means to provide students with access to high-quality education and the opportunity to succeed once they have been admitted. While some desegregation remedies meet the formal legal requirements of *Fordice*, they may not go far enough to deal with fundamental educational issues. Mississippi's new admission requirements eliminate one major vestige of the state's segregated past—multi-tiered, racially identifiable admission practices. One year after their initial implementation, however, both the number of first-year minority students and their representation in the system is significantly less than it was the year before and lower than it was the year after black citizens went to court to plead for a fairer system of higher education.

Sound educational practice suggests that policies that contribute to reduced minority access to higher education should be weighed against reasonable alternatives. Education leaders in Mississippi should closely monitor black freshmen enrollment for the next few years and, at the same time, work toward more comprehensive approaches to enhance access for all students. This means developing and articulating, in concert with elementary and secondary educators and representatives of the state's community college system, an understanding that what happens—and what does not happen—in K-12 education directly affects students' chances of matriculating in and graduating from a four-year institution. Closer cooperation and systemic collaboration should be at the core of Mississippi's efforts to increase the percentage of its black students who go to college.

Adopting this comprehensive approach requires both pragmatism and commitment. In recent years, we have seen proof of Mississippi's slowly developing pragmatism. As a result of citizen concern and court orders, it has decided not to eliminate two of its higher education institutions, has embraced race-sensitive measures to encourage both increased enrollment in traditionally white institutions by black students and a greater white presence at historically black universities, and has taken first steps to enhance programs at its historically black universities. The test of its commitment lies ahead—in reforming its education system in a way that will promote real opportunity for black students.

Notes

[1] 505 U.S. 717 (1992).

[2] Educationally sound remedies are those that promote a student's access to and success in the educational institution of his or her choice, strengthen learning and the quality of instruction, and foster a coherent state system of higher education. (See the discussion in *Knight v. Alabama,* 900 F. Supp. 272, 282–286).

[3] Southern Education Foundation, *Redeeming the American Promise: Report of the Panel on Educational Opportunity and Postsecondary Desegregation,* Atlanta, GA: Southern Education Foundation, 1995.

[4] *Ayers v. Allain,* 674 F. Supp. 1523 (N.D. Miss., 1987).

[5] 914 F. 2nd 676 (5th Cir., 1990 en banc).

[6] 505 U.S. 717 (1992).

[7] Slip. Op. No. 4:75 CV009-13-0 (N.D. Miss., March 7, 1995).

[8] Robert A. Kronley, William A. Butts, and Walter Washington, *Transformation Through Collaboration: Desegregating Higher Education in the Mississippi Delta* (March 1996).

[9] E. K. Fretwell et al., *A Report to the Mississippi Board of Trustees of the Institutions of Higher Learning* (November 1996).

[10] Michael T. Nettles, "Minority Access to Public Undergraduate Colleges and Universities in Selected Southern States" (Paper commissioned by the Southern Education Foundation for its Panel on Educational Opportunity and Postsecondary Desegregation, February 17, 1994).

[11] Mississippi Institutions of Higher Learning, Office of Planning and Budget (1997).

[12] 78 F. 3rd 932, *cert. denied,* 116 S. Ct. 2581 (1996).

[13] 116 F. 3d 1183 (5th Cir. 1997).

[14] Each applicant who does not meet Mississippi's new admission requirements for four-year institutions is now referred for screening to determine if, with remedial assistance in the summer prior to matriculation, the student can meet the demands of the freshman year. In 1996, of the 2,335 applicants who were referred for screening, 890 (38 percent) actually were screened. After screening, 173 of this group were deemed eligible for fall enrollment without the summer remedial program. Another 218 students enrolled in the summer program, with 204 completing it.

The 377 students who were thus found or made eligible for admission to four-year institutions through screening and remediation represent 16 percent of those referred for screening and 42 percent of the cohort that ultimately participated in the process. The 1996 experience strongly suggests that the effectiveness of screening in promoting access can be greatly enhanced by increasing the number of non-qualifying applicants who actually go through the process. Encouraging these students to persist will require collaboration between Mississippi's higher education and K-12 systems.

[15] Andy Kanengiser, "Ayers Case Settlement Talks Fizzle," *Clarion-Ledger,* September 17, 1997.

CHAPTER 7

Race and Testing in College Admissions

MICHAEL T. NETTLES, LAURA W. PERNA, AND CATHERINE M. MILLETT

Introduction

For over thirty years, colleges and universities throughout the United States have sought to expand access for underrepresented minorities. Affirmative action in admissions has been a central strategy in this effort, guided by the landmark 1978 U.S. Supreme Court decision in *Regents of the University of California v. Bakke.*

Although some minority groups remain grossly underrepresented, significant progress has been achieved at our nation's top colleges and universities. These gains, particularly for African Americans and Hispanics, are now directly threatened by the reversal of public policy and by court decisions (such as California's Proposition 209 and the Fifth Circuit's ruling in *Hopwood v. Texas*) that prohibit the consideration of race as a factor in admissions decisions and emphasize standardized test scores as the most accurate and fair measure of applicants' worthiness. An increasing reliance on test scores as the primary measure of academic potential will inevitably compound the already inequitable conditions that the most selective colleges face.

In the short run at least, colleges face a momentous choice: limit the weight of admissions test scores or lose their hard-won diversity. It is essential that policymakers understand the implications of this dilemma, forced on them in a political and legal environment where testing is seen as the best means of ensuring educational quality at the same time that the legal justifications for diversity are eroding.

In the long run, it is critical that higher education have a much richer description of the value of diversity for fulfilling its basic mission. Equally important is that educators and policymakers alike arrive at a deeper understanding of what test results do and do not mean. The large differences in average test scores among racial and ethnic groups reveal drastic inequalities that persist in U.S. society and education. Will these test results be used as a justification for denying access to those who have historically been excluded from the best schools, or will they inspire a serious effort to remedy the pervasive underlying inequalities in precollegiate education?

The Admissions Dilemma for Higher Education

The controversy over affirmative action policies in college admissions is largely concentrated at the nation's most selective four-year colleges and universities. Admission to most higher education institutions is not highly competitive. As enrollment of underrepresented populations rises, a growing number of minorities are seeking admission to more selective institutions because they perceive that their post-graduation benefits will be greater.

These selective colleges have tried to provide greater access for underrepresented minority students through affirmative action policies and by broadening the traditional academic criteria they use in making admissions decisions—high school grades, rank, and admissions test scores. The most selective colleges and universities in the United States now employ a broad array of admissions criteria, including extracurricular activities, personal circumstances, family history and education, geographic location of the family home, language spoken at home, athletic ability, letters of recommendation, and other factors, to achieve racial, ethnic, geographic, and other types of diversity in their entering freshmen classes. Admissions officers at these schools know that grade-point averages and test scores measure only certain kinds of achievement and potential, and that broader criteria are equally, and sometimes more, valid as indicators of students' potential contribution to the college community.

Despite the many kinds of student diversity that colleges pursue, and despite the well-established validity of broader admissions criteria, the public spotlight remains on race and testing. Critics attack affirmative action by arguing that traditional academic criteria are the only fair measures of applicants' merit. They charge that some white and Asian students with superior academic credentials are being unfairly denied admission in favor of less-prepared African-American and Hispanic applicants. They point out that blacks and Hispanics are more likely to drop out of college than whites and Asians. Some critics charge that affirmative action policies lead to higher costs and tuition increases to accommodate the needs of disadvantaged minority students.

Public debate about affirmative action has focused largely on these issues rather than on the historical context of discrimination and inequality in education, the record of progress in minority representation and achievement in the last decade, or the complex problem of testing and its relation to fairness in admissions.

Progress in Minority Representation

Between 1984 and 1994, America's predominantly white colleges and universities made substantial progress enrolling and awarding degrees to larger numbers of African-American and Hispanic students. During the same time, historically black colleges and universities (HBCUs) substantially increased the number of white students enrolling and earning degrees.

Despite this progress, African Americans and Hispanics continue to be underrepresented. Black undergraduate enrollment increased at predominantly white four-year colleges and universities by 33.5 percent, from 828,500 to 1,106,000, between 1984 and 1994 (see Figure 1). Although this

FIGURE 1 *Trends in African-American and Hispanic Undergraduate Enrollment at Non-HBCUs: Selected Years from 1976 to 1994*

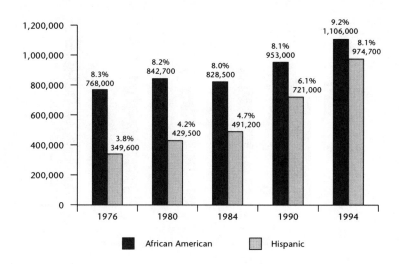

Source: Integrated Postsecondary Education Data System (IPEDS)

growth raised the representation of African Americans among undergraduates from 8.0 to 9.2 percent, the latter figure was still substantially below the percentage of African Americans in the nation's traditional college-age population (14.3 percent). Over this same period, Hispanic undergraduate enrollment increased at predominantly white colleges and universities by 98.4 percent, from 491,200 in 1984 to 974,700 in 1994. This increase brought Hispanic representation up to 8.1 percent of all undergraduates; nevertheless, Hispanics remained underrepresented relative to their numbers in the traditional college-age population (13.7 percent).

The number of bachelor's degrees awarded to African Americans by predominantly white schools increased by 42.8 percent, from 41,147 in 1984 to 58,749 in 1994 (see Figure 2). Nevertheless, African Americans represented only 4.3 percent of bachelor's degree recipients at white colleges and universities in 1984 and 5.1 percent in 1994. Similarly, the number of bachelor's degrees awarded to Hispanics by non-HBCUs increased by 91.3 percent, from 25,656 in 1984 to 49,073 in 1994. This growth raised the representation of Hispanics from 2.7 percent in 1984 to only 4.3 percent in 1994.

African-American and Hispanic enrollments have increased at all types of institutions, throughout the range of selectivity. But the largest and most

FIGURE 2 *Trends in the Number of Bachelor's Degrees Awarded to African Americans and Hispanics by Non-HBCUs: Selected Years from 1976 to 1994*

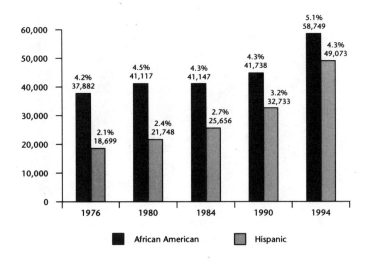

Source: Integrated Postsecondary Education Data System (IPEDS)

TABLE 1   *Change in Distribution of African-American and Hispanic Under-graduates Enrolled at 4-Year Colleges, by Carnegie Classification, 1984 to 1995*

		Total				
	1984		*1995*		*Change*	
Total	100%	5,877,034	100%	6,480,513	100%	603,479
Research I	23.8%	1,399,239	22.3%	1,450,743	8.5%	51,504
Research II	8.5%	502,009	7.7%	498,562	-0.6%	-3,447
Doctoral	15.0%	880,925	14.7%	955,482	12.4%	74,557
Comprehensive	38.2%	2,246,695	39.2%	2,546,593	49.7%	299,898
Liberal Arts	14.4%	848,166	15.9%	1,029,133	30.0%	180,967

		African-American				
Total	100%	484,022	100%	663,372	100%	179,350
Research I	16.4%	79,493	14.6%	96,905	9.7%	17,412
Research II	5.3%	25,666	4.6%	30,305	2.6%	4,639
Doctoral	14.7%	71,0321	4.9%	98,843	15.5%	27,811
Comprehensive	45.7%	221,148	46.5%	308,270	48.6%	87,122
Liberal Arts	17.9%	86,683	19.5%	129,049	23.6%	42,366

		Hispanic				
Total	100%	181,371	100%	376,431	100%	195,060
Research I	25.8%	46,749	22.5%	84,752	19.5%	38,003
Research II	5.0%	9,065	5.5%	20,775	6.0%	11,710
Doctoral	14.6%	26,531	14.6%	55,007	14.6%	28,476
Comprehensive	45.1%	81,768	47.2%	177,799	49.2%	96,031
Liberal Arts	9.5%	17,258	10.1%	38,098	10.7%	20,840

Note: Totals do not include students enrolled at specialized four-year colleges and universities.

competitive universities account for only a modest share of the increase. About one-half of the growth in four-year undergraduate enrollment between 1984 and 1995 occurred at so-called comprehensive universities for both African Americans and Hispanics (see Table 1). As a result of this growth, the percentage of African Americans enrolled at comprehensive institutions rose from 45.7 in 1984 to 46.5 in 1995; the corresponding percentage of Hispanics rose from 45.1 to 47.2. So-called Research I universities

TABLE 2 *Change in the Distribution of African-American and Hispanic Undergraduates Enrolled at 4-Year Colleges, by Institutional Selectivity, 1984 to 1995*

		Total				
	1984		1995		Change	
Total	100%	5,814,344	100%	6,455,371	100%	641,027
Most Competitive	3.2%	190,768	3.1%	201,259	1.6%	10,491
Highly Competitive	7.1%	414,540	6.6%	428,654	2.2%	14,114
Very Competitive	21.1%	1,225,293	20.3%	1,315,067	14.0%	89,774
Competitive	44.6%	2,592,311	45.2%	2,917,521	50.7%	325,210
Less Competitive	16.6%	963,336	17.0%	1,095,851	20.7%	132,515
Non-competitive	7.4%	428,096	7.7%	497,019	10.7%	68,923

		African-American				
Total	100%	476,889	100%	670,659	100%	193,770
Most Competitive	2.1%	10,093	1.8%	12,053	1.0%	1,960
Highly Competitive	3.4%	16,127	3.2%	21,599	2.8%	5,472
Very Competitive	12.8%	61,113	13.2%	88,830	14.3%	27,717
Competitive	40.9%	194,877	40.1%	269,011	38.3%	74,134
Less Competitive	28.3%	135,043	27.3%	183,367	24.9%	48,324
Non-competitive	12.5%	59,636	14.3%	95,799	18.7%	36,163

		Hispanic				
Total	100%	179,874	100%	372,747	100%	192,873
Most Competitive	3.0%	5,399	2.7%	9,976	2.4%	4,577
Highly Competitive	5.4%	9,820	6.2%	22,945	6.8%	13,125
Very Competitive	24.1%	43,314	25.5%	95,000	26.8%	51,686
Competitive	40.5%	72,806	38.8%	144,524	37.2%	71,718
Less Competitive	19.1%	34,288	18.9	70,621	18.8%	36,333
Non-competitive	7.9%	14,247	8.0%	29,681	8.0%	15,434

Note: Totals do not include students enrolled at specialized four-year colleges and universities. Institutional selectivity defined by Barron's *Profile of American Colleges.*

accounted for an additional 19.5 percent of the growth in Hispanic undergraduate enrollment and 9.7 percent of the growth in African-American undergraduate enrollment.

The share of Hispanics enrolled at Research I universities actually declined from 25.8 percent in 1984 to 22.5 percent in 1995, while the representation of African Americans declined from 16.4 to 14.6 percent. Almost one-fourth of the growth in African-American four-year undergraduate enrollment and more than 10 percent of the growth in Hispanic undergraduate enrollment occurred at liberal arts colleges. This raised the proportion of African Americans enrolled at liberal arts colleges from 17.9 percent in 1984 to 19.5 percent in 1995, and the proportion of Hispanics from 9.5 percent in 1984 to 10.1 percent in 1995.

Looking at institutional selectivity (as defined by Barron's *Profile of American Colleges*), more than one-third of the undergraduate enrollment growth for both African Americans (38.3 percent) and Hispanics (37.2 percent) occurred at "competitive" colleges and universities. The proportion of African Americans enrolled at these schools remained virtually unchanged between 1984 and 1995 (see Table 2). The proportion of Hispanics enrolled at "competitive" institutions fell from 40.5 percent in 1984 to 38.8 percent in 1995.

"Very competitive" institutions accounted for an additional 26.8 percent of the growth in Hispanic undergraduate enrollment and 14.3 percent of the growth in African-American undergraduate enrollment. The percentage of African Americans enrolled at "very competitive" colleges rose from 12.8 in 1984 to 13.2 in 1995, while the corresponding percentage of Hispanics rose from 24.1 to 25.5.

The "most competitive" and "highly competitive" campuses where the affirmative action issue is serious accounted for just 3.8 percent of the growth in African-American undergraduates and 9.2 percent of the growth in Hispanic undergraduates. In fact, the percentage of African Americans enrolled at these institutions actually declined from 5.5 in 1984 to 5.0 in 1995. Over the same period, the percentage of Hispanics enrolled at such schools increased from 8.4 to 8.9.

Increasing Reliance on Standardized Test Scores

Test scores play a prominent, if not a dominant, role among admissions criteria at highly selective colleges and universities. Most four-year public universities consider high school grades and test scores very important in making admissions decisions, according to surveys reported by the College Entrance Examination Board. Private doctoral-granting institutions and liberal arts institutions also attach great weight to these factors.

The effects of enforcing a minimum required test score and the weight assigned to test scores in deciding access and participation would appear to

TABLE 3 Admissions Criteria Rated Very Important, Fall 1994

| | Institutions | | | Percent | | | | | |
	In Universe	Number in Table	% of Universe	School Achievement	Test Scores	Interview	Recommen- dations	Activities	Essay
4-yr Public									
Ph.D. Granting	199	195	98.0%	97.9%	67.7%	1.6%	0.5%	0.5%	2.6%
Other Public	293	291	99.3%	91.4%	53.6%	1.7%	3.8%	1.4%	2.1%
All 4-yr Public	492	486	98.8%	94.0%	59.3%	1.7%	2.5%	1.0%	2.3%
4-yr Private									
Ph.D. Granting	154	153	99.4%	89.5%	40.5%	6.5%	11.8%	7.2%	11.8%
Liberal Arts	330	330	100.0%	98.5%	40.3%	5.8%	17.9%	2.7%	15.2%
Other Private I	196	193	98.5%	95.3%	47.2%	8.9%	13.5%	2.6%	7.8%
Other Private II	197	191	97.0%	78.0%	41.3%	15.9%	21.1%	5.3%	20.2%
Special pUrpose	242	237	97.9%	58.2%	28.9%	23.6%	32.3%	1.3%	22.5%
All 4-yr Private	1,119	1,104	98.7%	84.5%	39.9%	12.0%	19.9%	3.5%	15.8%
All 4-yr Institutions	1,611	1,590	98.7%	87.4%	45.4%	8.8%	14.6%	2.7%	11.7%

Source: The College Board, "Summary Statistics: Annual Survey of Colleges, 1995–96/1996–97."

Note: Universe does not include institutions with open admissions or upper-division institutions.

be greatest at more selective colleges and universities. To be given serious consideration at such schools, applicants must present acceptable test scores and grades in a college preparatory curriculum. Of the two, test scores are often perceived to be the most reliable, objective measure, although university admissions directors consistently report that they assign more weight to school achievement (see Table 3).

The average performance of African Americans and Hispanics on standardized tests is substantially lower than that of whites and Asians (see Figures 3 and 4). Trend data show that this gap has remained stable over several years.

Due to the vast statistical differences in average performance by race on standardized admissions tests, selective colleges and universities have adjusted the weight given to test scores in order to achieve racial and ethnic variety in their entering classes. As a result, African-American and Hispanic students enrolled in the most selective schools have lower average SAT and ACT scores than their white and Asian peers.

Removing the ability of admissions committees to make this kind of adjustment in the weighting of test scores might well be disastrous for blacks and Hispanics. The precise impact at highly selective public universities is not yet clear, but applying uniform admissions test requirements across all racial groups would without question dramatically reduce the number of eligible African Americans and Hispanics. The University of Michigan, for example, estimates that the number of African Americans in the 1995 entering freshman class would have dropped from 580 to fewer than 100 if admissions tests scores were used uniformly as the sole or dominant criterion.

Reconsidering the Role of Testing

Regardless of the standardized test used, a smaller percentage of African Americans and Hispanics fall into the high end of the score distribution than of whites and Asians. Thus, a very small number of African Americans and Hispanics would be admitted to the most selective institutions if test scores were the dominant criterion.

Of 210,076 African Americans and 164,142 Hispanics taking the 1996 SAT, 58.2 percent of the African Americans and 46.3 percent of the Hispanics scored in the lowest quartile (see Table 4). Only 5.5 percent of the African Americans and 10.2 percent of the Hispanics placed in the highest quartile. Only 25,406 (12.1 percent) African Americans and 33,246 (20.3 percent) Hispanics achieved a combined score of 1100 or higher, compared to 563,739 (41.4 percent) of whites.

FIGURE 3   *Trends in Verbal and Math Mean Scores of Students Taking the SAT*

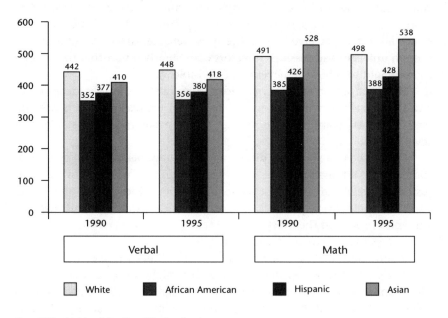

Unpublished tables, Educational Testing Service

What accounts for this gap? One factor, often overlooked by higher education policymakers, is the persisting inequities in precollege education. Another factor is unequal access to test-specific preparation, provided both by schools and businesses, which have been shown to affect performance significantly.

We will not address here the complex issue of the reliability of standardized tests in predicting academic success. But we must reiterate what admissions officers at virtually every selective college and, indeed, the testmakers themselves point out: that high performance on these tests is not the only measure of academic achievement or predictor of academic success.

The data above suggest that, where affirmative action is prohibited, colleges and universities may have to consider both a short-term and a long-term strategy to maintain or increase diversity on their campuses. In the short term, they must choose between de-emphasizing test scores and losing their diversity. Institutions must become more cognizant of other measures of academic achievement and take into account the unequal preparation available to different applicants. Universities also need to become more actively involved in improving the preparation students receive before college.

One example of a short-term strategy is the University of Michigan's undergraduate admissions process. Test scores and grade point averages together continue to have high priority, with about 70 percent of the weight placed on grades in college preparatory high school courses and 30 percent on test scores. Then, the university examines additional criteria for each applicant who has acceptable high school grades and test scores. These include quality of the high school, rigor of the high school curriculum, unusual talents, geographic diversity, and alumni relatives.

Average test scores of students admitted to the University of Michigan vary across racial and ethnic groups. In 1995, the average total SAT score (verbal and math combined) for applicants who were admitted to and enrolled at the university was 1251, compared with 1123 for underrepresented minorities (1084 for African Americans, 1189 for Hispanics, and

FIGURE 4 *Trends in Verbal and Quantitative Mean Scores of Students Taking the Graduate Record Examination*

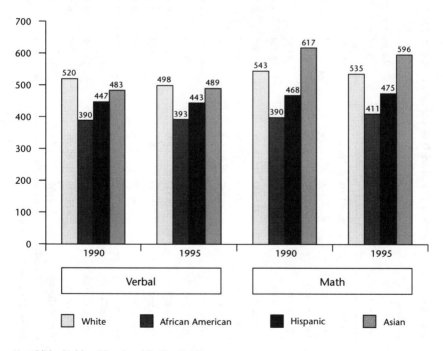

Unpublished tables, Educational Testing Service

TABLE 4 Recentered 1996 SAT Score Distribution by Race and Sex

SAT Score Range	White		African American		Hispanic		Asian American	
	Total	%	Total	%	Total	%	Total	%
Total	1,362,216	100.0%	210,076	100.0%	164,142	100.0%	168,588	100.0%
1500 to 1600	22,624	1.7%	344	0.2%	761	0.5%	6,521	3.9%
1400 to 1490	48,291	3.5%	1,035	0.5%	1,777	1.1%	10,442	6.2%
1300 to 1390	99,304	7.3%	2,980	1.4%	4,505	2.7%	15,243	9.0%
1200 to 1290	168,873	12.4%	7,159	3.4%	9,693	5.9%	20,601	12.2%
1100 to 1190	224,647	16.5%	13,888	6.6%	16,510	10.1%	23,064	13.7%
1000 to 1090	252,463	18.5%	24,177	11.5%	23,766	14.5%	23,875	14.2%
900 to 990	244,042	17.9%	38,138	18.2%	31,191	19.0%	23,471	13.9%
800 to 890	164,904	12.1%	44,085	21.0%	30,328	18.5%	18,368	10.9%
700 to 790	86,802	6.4%	39,693	18.9%	23,782	14.5%	12,985	7.7%
600 to 690	34,857	2.6%	21,832	10.4%	13,213	8.0%	7,608	4.5%
500 to 590	10,971	0.8%	11,154	5.3%	5,747	3.5%	4,068	2.4%
400 to 490	4,438	0.3%	5,591	2.7%	2,869	1.7%	2,342	1.4%
Lowest Quartile	301,972	22.2%	122,355	58.2%	75,939	46.3%	45,371	26.9%
Second Quartile	244,042	17.9%	38,138	18.2%	31,191	19.0%	23,471	13.9%
Third Quartile	477,110	35.0%	38,065	18.1%	40,276	24.5%	46,939	27.8%
Highest Quartile	339,092	24.9%	11,518	5.5%	16,736	10.2%	52,807	31.3%

Source: Educational Testing Service

1178 for American Indians), 1289 for Asians, and 1269 for whites (see Table 5). The comparable ACT scores were 27.2 overall, 23.6 for underrepresented minorities (22.6 for African Americans, 25.9 for Hispanics, and 26.0 for American Indians), 27.6 for Asians, and 27.9 for whites.

These differences in test scores have not prevented the University of Michigan from maintaining its standards of academic excellence. Indeed, they are a sign of its commitment to a fair representation of minority students.

Implications for Further Research

The push for greater reliance on test scores in college admissions comes before we know completely how much the use of alternative admissions criteria has contributed to increasing access for underrepresented minorities. The extent to which affirmative action contributes to the progress African Americans, Latinos, American Indians, and whites have made attending and receiving degrees at colleges and universities where they are members of the minority racial group has not been adequately evaluated. Additional research and analysis is needed in order to articulate the costs and benefits of admissions policies that seek to achieve greater racial diversity, and to examine the consequences of these admissions policies for majority and minority students.

These legal challenges to the university admissions process threaten the progress of the past decade in increasing diversity. Universities are unable to forecast the effects of these changes or to find viable alternatives. Research should address the following questions:

- What is the impact of admissions standards, such as minimum test scores, on racial and ethnic diversity in selective colleges and universities?
- What are the benefits to colleges and universities, to their students, and to society of having a racially and ethnically diverse student body?
- What are the effects of affirmative action admissions policies on access and degree completion rates of minorities?
- What have colleges and universities learned about the effects of their admissions processes and standards that can be used to improve the graduation rates of underrepresented minority students?
- What actions should colleges and universities be taking to improve the performance of minorities on important admissions criteria?

TABLE 5 *Average SAT and ACT Scores for Freshman Class, University of Michigan, 1996*

	SAT Total Score	ACT Composite Score
All Freshmen	1251	27.2
Underrepresented Minorities	1123	23.6
Blacks	1084	22.6
Hispanics	1189	25.9
American Indians	1178	26.0
Asian Americans	1289	27.6
White	1269	27.9

Source: Unpublished undergraduate admissions data

The answers to these questions will help educators respond to the critics of current admissions policies and also reduce the need for different policies for underrepresented minorities in the future.

Conclusion

President Clinton's support for national tests and standards as central components of elementary and secondary education reform illustrates the confidence that policymakers have in standardized testing. The popular view is that tests are the best way to measure learning. In this context, it is doubtful that colleges and universities will be able to continue applying different thresholds and weights to the test scores of applicants of different racial and ethnic groups.

The implications of this fact are, to put it bluntly, frightening. The substantially lower average scores of African Americans and Hispanics on standardized tests like the SAT mean that uniform treatment of test scores will inevitably reduce the presence of African Americans and Hispanics on the campuses of selective colleges and universities. As a result, the progress that has been achieved over the past decade in raising the representation of African Americans and Hispanics may well be at an end, and the still large gap between blacks' and Hispanics' representation in college and their proportions in the population will grow even larger.

CHAPTER 8

Testing a New Approach to Admissions: The Irvine Experience

SUSAN WILBUR AND
MARGUERITE BONOUS-HAMMARTH

Introduction

On July 20, 1995, the Regents of the University of California (UC) voted to eliminate affirmative action in admissions, hiring, and contractual agreements. The new policy on undergraduate admissions, Resolution SP-1, banned the use of race, religion, sex, color, ethnicity, or national origin as criteria for admission to the university or to any program of study. Following this decision, a task force of university faculty, administrators, and students met to discuss and propose new guidelines for undergraduate admissions that would conform to the requirements of Resolution SP-1.

Under the Regents' decision, now reinforced by California's Proposition 209,[1] University of California campuses are restricted to the use of nonracial standards in all admissions decisions. This paper describes the early experiences of one campus—the University of California, Irvine (UCI)—in developing and implementing admissions criteria consistent with the new guidelines. As admissions officers at UCI, we were especially interested in documenting the effects of the new criteria on racial diversity in the freshman class.

Our results demonstrate an overwhelming need to reconceptualize the university admissions process if we hope to maintain diversity in the student body.

A Troubling Decline in Applicants

Although Resolution SP-1 does not go into effect until 1998, the Regents' vote and the passage of Proposition 209 appear to have had a chilling effect on the aspirations of some prospective UC students. These two highly publicized votes are not the only possible explanation for the subsequent decline in the number of African-American, Chicano, Latino, and American Indian applicants, but it seems clear that they were at least an important contributing factor.

The overall number of UC applications for the fall 1997 term increased by 5 percent over the preceding year.[2] Applications from Filipino Americans, Asian Americans, and Caucasians increased, while applications from African Americans, American Indians, Chicanos, and Latinos went down.

The pattern at UCI mirrored that of the system as a whole. From fall 1996 to fall 1997 there was a 4 percent increase in applications from California high school seniors. Adding the 5 percent increase from the preceding year, this represented a 9 percent overall increase in the number of freshman applicants to UCI from fall 1995 to fall 1997. Gains occurred primarily among Asian-American and Caucasian applicants (8 percent and 2 percent, respectively). During this same two-year period there were dramatic declines in applications from underrepresented ethnic groups: a 13 percent drop among African Americans, a 13 percent decline among Chicanos, a 10 percent decrease among Latinos, and a 12 percent drop among American Indians.

In this increasingly competitive admissions environment, only 5 percent of African-American and 4 percent of Chicano/Latino high school graduates are among the top 12.5 percent of all California graduates who are eligible for admission to UC.[3] With such a small pool of eligible students to begin with, any decline in the number of underrepresented minority applicants is troubling.

UC Irvine's Response to SP-1

The discussion of new admissions guidelines was informed by the university's mission and responsibilities as defined in California's Master Plan of Higher Education. It specifies that the top one-eighth of the state's public high school graduates be eligible for admission to UC. The discussion was further guided by the tradition of public service originating in the university's land grant status, and by the purposes and demands of undergraduate programs within the context of the university's research environment.

Prior to the implementation of the new SP-1 guidelines, UCI admissions procedures were relatively formulaic. Each application was reviewed first for minimum UC eligibility. Then every student was assigned a selection index—a number representing his or her grade point average (GPA) and required test scores (SAT Verbal, SAT Mathematics, and three SAT II exams). In addition, applications were reviewed for the number and quality of courses completed and for supplemental criteria, including special talents and circumstances that may have adversely affected the applicant's life, such as disabilities, personal difficulties, low family income, and ethnic identity. But the greatest emphasis was placed on the selection index number. Applicants received only one review, and considerably less weight was given to such factors as leadership, honors and awards, and other accomplishments that might serve as evidence of potential contribution to the campus community.

Following release of the new selection guidelines in July 1996, faculty and administrators—and, in some cases, students—at each campus met to develop campus-specific responses. At UCI, lengthy discussions led to the adoption of principles to guide admissions practices. Two of these principles are especially important.

First, the faculty wished to ensure that, at the freshman level, UCI would continue to select students from the entire range of eligible applicants. This principle was critical. In the event that UCI attracted more UC-eligible applicants than could be admitted—as was in fact the case for fall 1997—campus policy would allow the admissions office to select students from among the entire eligible pool rather than to narrowly limit admission to applicants with the highest grade point averages or test scores. This principle allows for the consideration of well-rounded students who have demonstrated both academic and co-curricular talents.[4]

A second principle—that merit is demonstrated in many forms and measured in different ways—opened the door for a more comprehensive review process, and allowed for consideration of such factors as leadership, initiative, ability to overcome personal hardships, and potential contributions to the campus. Informed by a small research project using alternative assessment methods for freshmen admission conducted at UCI between 1993 and 1997, and rooted in Gardner's (1993) theory of multiple intelligences, this principle acknowledged the value of traditional measures like grades and test scores, but affirmed the validity of other kinds of accomplishments, distinctive to each applicant, as part of the admissions process.

Collectively, these principles led to the design and implementation of a new, comprehensive UCI admissions process for fall 1997.

UCI's New Admissions Process

UCI implemented a two-step freshman application review, in which we examined every applicant's academic and personal profiles. The academic profile included evidence of academic achievement: self-reported GPA, required test scores, total number of courses including approved honors and college-level courses completed, and total number of courses projected to be completed during the 12th grade. Applicants were grouped by similarity of their academic profiles. For fall 1997, 60 percent of the UCI freshman class was selected on the strength of the academic profile alone.[5] The other 40 percent of the class was selected on the basis of academic *and* personal profiles.

The personal profile included evidence of the applicant's curricular, co-curricular, or experiential skills, knowledge, and abilities that might contribute to success at UCI. The task of reading and scoring applications required special procedures to produce equitable and consistent results. All admissions staff involved in undergraduate outreach and evaluation participated in training about the personal profile criteria, including discussions about evaluating evidence in different parts of the application and personal statement and practice in using multiple criteria to assign one personal profile score per applicant. These training sessions began in December and continued throughout the reading period.

Approximately 7,500 freshman applicants who were not selected solely on the strength of their academic profiles received at least two double-blind readings of their applications, for a total of 15,000 individual reviews. Computer reports were generated to identify applicants whose two personal profile scores were more than one point apart. There were 862 such applicants. Their applications were reviewed by a third staff member, whose score was considered final. From this total cohort of 7,500, just over 4,100 applicants were offered admission.

This work was done by 23 readers—nine admissions counselors, ten outreach counselors, and four senior managers. In previous years, freshman selection was done by ten admissions counselors. The time frame remained the same, with most admissions decisions made during the intense seven-week period between mid-January and March 1, but the workload was obviously much increased.

No additional financial resources were provided to support this effort, and we were not able to authorize overtime pay. The staff was therefore hard-pressed to meet the March 1 deadline. We believed, however, that a comprehensive review process would be the best way to choose UCI's freshman class, and considered the significant additional investment of staff time necessary.

Each personal profile score reflected seven factors: leadership and initiative, honors and awards, personal challenges, geographic challenges (including the quality of the academic profile relative to available educational opportunities), self-awareness (that is, evidence of active commitment based on self-identified values), civic and cultural awareness, and specialized knowledge.

The personal profile criteria and review process reflect a conscious effort to link theory and practice. We know from the literature on involvement theory (Astin, 1991) that students who become socialized and involved in their education are more likely to succeed. Evidence of an applicant's activities, service, and awards illustrates breadth and depth of involvement. At the same time, we acknowledge that not all students know how to become involved in activities, while others have outside commitments that preclude extensive involvement, such as the need to work to support self and family. For this reason, multiple criteria were used in assessing the personal profiles.

The self-assessment concept is perhaps the least well known of the personal profile attributes. Self-assessment has been linked in the leadership and student development literature to the goals of collegiate education: the development of leadership and talent, the enhancement of creativity, and the fostering of citizenship and service to others (Covey, 1991; Higher Education Research Institute, 1996; Rogers, 1980; Senge, 1990). It is not uncommon for an applicant to articulate skills, strengths, and well-developed interests in his or her personal statement; this information can, in turn, be used to gain perspective on the applicant's potential for success at the university and potential contribution to the campus community.

The Results of UCI's New Admissions Process

How did the new admissions process work? Specifically, what impact did it have on the ethnic diversity of the freshman class in fall 1997? To answer these questions, we first looked at the racial and ethnic makeup of the applicant pool.

All 17,183 UCI applicants completed the official UC application, which includes a question about ethnic identity. The largest cohorts were Caucasian, Chinese/Chinese American, Korean, Chicano, and Filipino. Of the total applicant pool, 13,925 (81 percent) met UC academic eligibility requirements (see Table 1).[6]

TABLE 1 *Racial/Ethnic Background of Freshman Applicants to UCI, Fall 1997*

| | All Applicants | | UC-Eligible Applicants | |
	N	% of Total	N	% of Total
Caucasian	4,193	24.4 ·	3,503	25.6
Chinese	3,238	18.8	2,644	19.3
Korean	1,673	9.7	1,268	9.3
Chicano	1,549	9.0	1,105	8.1
Filipino	1,239	7.2	1,057	7.7
Vietnamese	1,155	6.7	991	7.2
East Indian/Pakistani	679	4.0	549	4.0
Other Asian	613	3.6	478	3.5
Latino	568	3.3	401	2.9
African American	552	3.2	317	2.3
Japanese	489	2.8	390	2.8
American Indian	89	.5	61	.4
Pacific Islander	70	.4	51	.4
Ethnicity Unknown	1,076	6.3	892	6.5
Total	17,183	100.0	13,707	100.0

Source: UCI Office of Admissions and Relations with Schools

To judge the impact of the fall 1997 admissions process on ethnic diversity, we compared the actual makeup of the newly admitted freshman class with the hypothetical makeup of a class admitted solely on the basis of the academic selection index—that is, by a ranking system based on GPA and test scores. It is important to note that, even under the old, more formulaic system, UCI did not admit students only on the basis of grade point averages and test scores. Other information, like honors and awards, was given some consideration. Nevertheless, this preliminary analysis offers a gross comparison that is useful.

The comparison shows that the use of expanded selection criteria in the personal profile resulted in significant gains for underrepresented ethnic groups—particularly African Americans, American Indians, and Chicanos (see Table 2).

The gains noted for certain ethnic groups in this comparison could result because eligible students from these cohorts tended to be distributed more broadly across academic majors. (Actual admissions decisions are affected by applicants' choice of major and the number of available slots in the various academic programs.) By the same token, the numbers of Chinese and Korean applicants actually admitted may be lower because of their concentration in majors that are more constrained on the campus, or because of other factors weighed in the admissions decision, such as level of involvement in co-curricular activities.

The probability of admission was lower for applicants in information and computer science, biological science, and unaffiliated categories than in other areas. On the other hand, applicants in the arts, where there was greater enrollment capacity in 1997, had a higher chance of admission than other applicants in this data set. These results suggest that enrollment targets and availability of majors play important roles in selection outcomes.

The findings strongly suggest, however, that the consideration of more comprehensive criteria in the academic and personal profiles had a significant impact on admissions decisions. In general, freshman admission to UCI for fall 1997 was the most selective in campus history. Of more than 17,000 applicants, 66 percent were offered admission. The more compre-

TABLE 2 *Comparison of Hypothetical UCI Admits (Academic Index Only) with Actual Admits, by Race/Ethnicity, Fall 1997*

	Hypothetical	Actual	% Change
African American	174	226	+29.9
American Indian	45	56	+24.4
Chicano	676	821	+21.4
Latino	297	320	+7.7
Other Asian	330	353	+7.0
Vietnamese	704	727	+3.3
East Indian/Pakistani	444	454	+2.3
Caucasian	2,723	2,771	+1.8
Filipino	751	748	−.4
Pacific Islander	32	31	−3.1
Japanese	314	302	−3.8
Chinese	2,185	1,983	−9.2
Korean	1,025	920	−10.2
Ethnicity Unknown	696	684	−1.7
Total	10,396	10,396	0.0

hensive selection criteria were vital tools used to admit students who showed progressive academic accomplishment and potential for success at UCI.

Moreover, without the use of explicit racial standards, the new criteria resulted in the admission of a freshman class of approximately the same racial and ethnic composition as the fall 1996 entering class. The percentage of Chicano (7 percent), Latino (3 percent), and white (26 percent) students in the fall 1997 pool of admitted students remained the same as in the year before. African Americans (3 percent) increased by one percentage point, while Asian Americans (52 percent) declined slightly more than one percentage point. More important, however, is the fact that these admitted freshmen will presumably show a proclivity for greater involvement and participation in academic and social life on campus because of the increased emphasis on these factors in the admissions process.

What We Learned

The most important lesson we learned is that it is possible for a selective university to admit an academically well-prepared and diverse freshman class without the use of race or ethnicity as a factor in the review process. It is important to understand, however, that no one model can predict selection outcomes from year to year. Changes in application numbers and the enrollment needs of specific programs are just two factors that can influence these outcomes.

Several challenging issues emerged during the 1997 review process. First, our preliminary planning was based on simulation models derived from the fall 1996 freshman applicant pool. While we anticipated an increase in the number of freshman applicants for 1997 because of the increasing number of students graduating from California high schools, we did not adequately anticipate the increase in the academic quality of these applicants. GPAs, test scores, and the number of academic courses completed in high school were all up. This increase resulted in more than 60 percent of the applicant pool being coded initially for academic selection.

This required us to adjust the academic criteria in the middle of the review process, resulting in approximately 1,000 additional applicants needing a personal profile review fairly late in the process—a significant additional workload for an already overworked staff. We should have planned more varied scenarios, run more simulations during the planning phase, and built in more flexibility and time. Prior to the fall 1998 cycle, we will review the academic criteria that led to the selection of the fall 1997 class and develop a more refined model for identifying the top 60 percent of the pool.

Second, we discovered that it was difficult for staff members to adjust to the idea that some applicants who would have been considered "academic admits" in previous years were not as highly rated in this cycle and, in some cases, were not even offered admission. Applicants not selected in the first 60 percent were subject to the personal profile review. Sometimes the decision hung on whether the application and personal statement were done thoroughly and completely.

One applicant, for example, who had a 3.89 GPA, strong academic preparation, and a 1270 combined SAT verbal and math score did not meet the criteria for selection in the first 60 percent. This applicant did not complete the honors and awards, extracurricular activities, community service work, or employment sections of the application, and her personal statement provided little useful information. She was not selected for admission.

This example illustrates a tension that may emerge during the selection process. As admissions professionals, we have grown accustomed to using high academic achievement as the single best criterion for admission. Knowing that a particular applicant would likely have been admitted under a narrow system that considered only academic achievements, some staff members balk at the idea of turning that student down on the basis of "softer" criteria. We needed to have extensive conversations about the outcomes we were trying to achieve through this process. The fact that the faculty committee had articulated the principle that UCI would continue to select students from the entire range of the top one-eighth of students served as a useful tool in helping staff understand the purpose of the comprehensive review process.

Third, the reading of files went very slowly at first, but picked up speed as staff became more comfortable with the criteria and process. All admissions and outreach staff were diverted to the review of high school applicants, delaying the review of transfer applicants. Across the board, staff expressed a need for even more training and practice, as well as time to deal with other pressing responsibilities. We also need to build in time simply to take a breather from the intensity of the reading.

We plan to continue with an aggressive plan of self-evaluation, looking particularly for ways to streamline the process—especially by using technology to expedite the more mechanical aspects of the review. We are also discussing the possibility of including UCI faculty, high school counselors and teachers, and UCI staff in related professional areas (such as academic counselors and student support staff) in our pool of readers.

Implications and Limitations

Consistent with previous research on the importance of broader academic and personal criteria in college admissions, our findings suggest that a more comprehensive review of applicants' abilities is advantageous to students in underrepresented ethnic groups (Willingham, 1985). As college administrators and faculty, we should strive to admit students who will meet not only institutional objectives for learning but also the larger goals of personal and community growth as students and alumni.

Institutions as well as individuals affect undergraduates' learning, leadership development, and other social and cognitive skills (Astin, 1993; Willingham, 1985; Higher Education Research Institute, 1996). Admissions decisions consider precollege evidence of academic accomplishment that match the profile of current successful undergraduates on campus. In this sense, institutions with diverse enrollments of academically talented and involved students will contribute to the development of their undergraduates by offering a supportive environment and opportunities for positive student-peer and student-faculty interaction. Further, students coming to college with such "multiple intelligences" may add greater depth and direction to one another's learning.

Admissions decisions are not made in a vacuum. Admissions officials are pressured by deadlines, by workload and budget constraints, and by shifting campus priorities, enrollment capacities, and interests of applicants. The results of one year's experience cannot effectively predict long-term outcomes. Rather, it will take careful planning, revision, and testing of new admissions models to achieve effective enrollment management processes for a campus.

The UCI experience in developing and implementing new selection criteria will ultimately be tested by the long-term outcomes for students. We must follow these students' achievements, social and cognitive growth, and retention rates. But we believe that they will take initiative, actively participate in their learning, and come equipped with diverse skills that will have a positive impact on their learning and the learning of others.

References

Astin, A. (1991). *Assessment for excellence: The philosophy and practice of assessment and evaluation in higher education.* San Francisco: Jossey-Bass.

Astin, A. (1993). *What matters in college?* San Francisco: Jossey-Bass.

California Postsecondary Education Commission. (1992). *Eligibility of California's high school graduates for 1990 admission to the state's public universities* (Commission Report No. 92-14). San Francisco: Author.

Covey, S. R. (1991). *Principle-centered learning*. New York: Summit Books.

Douglass, J. (1997). *Setting the conditions of undergraduate admissions: The role of University of California faculty in policy and process. A report to the Task Force on Governance*. New York: Basic Books.

Gardner, H. (1993). *Multiple intelligences: The theory in practice*. New York: Basic Books.

Higher Education Research Institute. (1996). *A social change model of leadership development*. Los Angeles: Author.

Rogers, C. (1980). *A way of being*. Boston: Houghton Mifflin.

Senge, P. (1990). *The fifth discipline: The art and practice of learning organizations*. New York: Doubleday Currency.

University of California. (1997). *Report on fall 1997 undergraduate applications*. Oakland: University of California, Office of the President.

Willingham, W. W. (1985). *Success in college: The role of personal qualities and academic ability*. New York: College Entrance Examination Board.

Notes

[1] Proposition 209 bans preferential treatment for any person or group in public employment, education, or contracting.

[2] The University of California receives applications in November for enrollment the following fall. Students can apply to more than one UC campus with a single application. A total of 54,000 students applied for fall 1997 admission. Applicants are asked their ethnic identity, with the following choices: "African-American/Black," "Mexican/Mexican-American/Chicano," "Other Spanish-American/Latino," "American Indian/Alaska Native," "Filipino/Filipino-American," "Vietnamese/Vietnamese-American," "Chinese/Chinese-American," "East Indian/Pakistani," "Japanese/Japanese-American," "Korean/Korean-American," "Pacific Islander," "Other Asian," "White/Caucasian," or "Other." Statistics quoted from University of California, 1997.

[3] California Postsecondary Education Commission, 1992.

[4] For a historical perspective on UC's commitment to diversity, see Douglass (1997).

[5] University-wide policy guidelines stipulate that at least 40 percent and no more than 60 percent of freshmen be admitted on the basis of academic criteria alone. Although there are some local variations by academic school or specific discipline, all UC campuses are currently selecting at least 50 percent of their freshman admits on academic criteria only. The UCI faculty has traditionally favored the 60 percent figure, believing that previous academic performance is the best indicator of future academic success.

[6] Total of eligible applicants in Table 1 is 13,707 because 218 students were admitted on additional criteria not included in this study.

CHAPTER 9

An Admissions Process for a Multiethnic Society

GREG TANAKA, MARGUERITE BONOUS-HAMMARTH, AND ALEXANDER W. ASTIN

Introduction: Two Essential Questions

Since the 1960s, higher education policymakers throughout the United States have been trying to create more inclusive institutional cultures by altering policies for student activities, residence life, curriculum, and admissions. At its 1997 annual meeting, the Association of American Universities, which represents 62 leading research institutions, called for continued attention to diversity, particularly in university admissions.

Such efforts have become increasingly controversial at many schools. Underlying the controversy is a fundamental disagreement about the value of diversity itself. Is creating and maintaining a racially and ethnically diverse community a legitimate goal for institutions of higher learning? While most university administrators and policymakers believe it is, many critics— and an increasing number of courts—are questioning this assumption.

In this essay we address two difficult but essential questions: First, does diversity have a benefit? And second, if diversity *is* important, how can the college admissions process help create diverse campuses, in light of recent court decisions on affirmative action admissions and nonracial standards?

The Changing Face of Universities

First, we must recognize that racial diversity is already a fact on many campuses. U.S. colleges are in rapid transition, particularly in multiracial communities where whites are, or will soon be, just one of several minorities. The proportion of students of color on U.S. campuses rose from 15.7 percent in 1976 to 24.6 percent in 1994.[1] College students in such communities must interact often and on many levels with students of different ethnic and racial backgrounds.

This transition is even more advanced in multiethnic states like California, where students of color in colleges and universities increased from 21.5 percent to 41.6 percent between 1979 and 1995.[2] Students of color now outnumber white students by a large margin on the University of California campuses at Berkeley, Los Angeles, and Irvine.

This increasing diversity on campus has led to a change in the way students of different cultures relate to each other. Traditional models of student development have not adjusted to these changing demographics. The old construct of "dominant" and "minority" cultures, in which educators have often evaluated the ability of students of color to fit in on a Eurocentric campus, is no longer adequate (Murgia, Padilla, and Pavel, 1991).

Educators commonly see students of color as "minorities" who must adapt to the dominant white culture, whereas white students, they assume, will easily fit in. But on truly multiracial campuses, this model of student development does an injustice to students of all ethnicities (Tanaka, 1996a, 1997).

How White Students Experience Multiracial Campuses

To answer our first question—Does diversity have a benefit?—we looked at the ways white students say they are affected by their experience of multiracial campuses. The data are from longitudinal surveys of 25,000 students at 159 colleges and universities.[3] We know from the work of Alexander Astin that students' learning is linked to the quality of their personal involvement in the campus community (Astin, 1975). Our findings build on Astin's further research showing that students' overall satisfaction with the undergraduate experience is enhanced when colleges put a high priority on diversity and multiculturalism (Astin, 1993). Was this reported increase in satisfaction an automatic result of increased campus diversity, or did other factors enter the equation?

The surveys asked students how their satisfaction with college and their sense of campus community were affected by multicultural experiences. We were especially interested in personal experiences that might be subject to at least partial control through institutional policy and practice. In particular, we wanted to know if a white student's response to an institution's efforts to promote multiculturalism depends on the nature of that student's direct experience with diverse peers.[4]

We found that white students on multicultural campuses reported increased satisfaction with their college experience when they participated in cross-cultural activities, defined as enrolling in an ethnic studies course, attending a racial/cultural awareness workshop, or socializing with someone from a different racial/ethnic group (see Table 1).

Moreover, using multiple regression analysis to control for differences in entering freshmen characteristics, we found that white students at colleges that gave a high priority to multiculturalism were significantly more satisfied with their college experience if they participated in cross-cultural activities.[5]

At the same time, this increase in satisfaction was erased for the subset of white students who were members of social fraternities or sororities, which tend to be highly segregated (see Table 2). Thus, emphasizing multiculturalism had positive effects only among students who did not join fraternities or sororities.[6]

The data suggest that white students' involvement in fraternities or sororities *conditions* their response to institutional policies to create a more diverse environment. These data are also consistent with findings in psychological research that "contact" alone will do little to promote positive change in racial attitudes across groups (Allport, 1954/1979). In short, we found that there are benefits from diversity, but they are not automatic.

TABLE 1 *Effect* of Three Dependent Variables on "Sense of Community" as Perceived by White Students*

	Among Students Who Engaged in One or More Cross-Cultural Activities (N=10,394)	Among Students Who Did Not Engage in Cross-Cultural Activities (N=6,536)
Creating a Multicultural Environment	.11**	.02
Faculty Racial Diversity	−.06**	−.04
Student Racial Diversity	−.10**	−.07**

* Standardized partial regression coefficients (Betas).

**Signifies p < .001

Note: Faculty racial diversity was measured by the percentage of full-time faculty of color as reported by the institution in the U.S. Department of Education 1989 IPEDS survey. Student racial diversity was computed by aggregating data for the percentages of black, Asian-American, and Latino students in the 1989 CIRP follow-up survey for each campus.

TABLE 2   *College Satisfaction for White Students, by Activities*

	N	b
Participated in One or More Cross-Cultural Activities	10,475	.06**
Did Not Participate in Cross-Cultural Activities	6,602	.03
Joined a Social Fraternity/Sorority	4,866	.03
Did Not Join a Fraternity/Sorority	12,635	.07**

**p < .001

Sense of Community: Cautionary Evidence

A second set of analyses from our study examined the impact of multiculturalism on white students' sense of campus community. We found that increasing numbers of students of color[7] and faculty of color[8] on campus was associated with a slightly weakened sense of community for white students, even those who had participated in cross-cultural activities as defined above. This is cause for concern. The findings suggest, among other things, that white students may have more difficulty feeling connected to a campus when the campus experiences an influx of students of color or faculty of color, which could be the result of the high level of segregation in pre-collegiate education.

A better understanding of students' development on multicultural campuses is needed. A recent report by Duster (1997) reveals that white students and students of color enter elite public colleges in California with very different expectations about multiculturalism: white students want to establish friendships with students of color, but students of color want to learn more about their own cultural identities and want to be affiliated with ethnic studies centers. Duster argues that colleges and universities must do more to meet both sets of expectations.

Traditional higher education policies need to be revised to reflect the critical roles of students in building a sense of community on multiethnic campuses. In particular, college administrators ought to examine the rationale for tolerating campus institutions—like fraternities and sororities—that further segregation in housing. We also believe it is essential to go beyond test scores and grades in the admissions process, and that it is appropriate to ask what aptitudes and experiences entering students might have that would predict successful leadership in a multiethnic society.

A New Role for Admissions: Promoting Cross-Cultural Learning

In the current debate about race and affirmative action, the process of college admission is usually seen as an issue of individual rights: does one particular student deserve to be admitted over some other particular student? But in choosing from a pool of applicants, admissions officers must consider the needs of the university as a community, not just individual needs.

The top colleges have recognized this fact for a long time and have developed subtle and complex criteria for selecting students. Such criteria should be more widely used, not just at elite schools but at any school that strives to prepare students for participation in a multiracial society.

We must find new ways of thinking about these issues; to do that, we need a better understanding of what multiculturalism means for white students. Minority outreach and affirmative action admissions programs were originally conceived as ways to bring successful students of color onto overwhelmingly white campuses. Although colleges considered diversity an asset, they rarely evaluated white applicants' experience of diversity or preparation to adjust to and contribute to a diverse community.

Higher education must teach all students skills that will enable them to become leaders in multiethnic societies when they graduate. Students lacking positive cross-cultural experiences in college who subsequently find themselves in multiethnic situations will be less able to manage their relations with others than those who develop skill in interacting with a diverse population.

College applicants who have lived and worked in multiracial communities and schools and reflected thoughtfully about those experiences represent an asset that could appropriately be considered in the admissions process. Many students of color have such experience: mobility in mainstream society for students from disadvantaged minorities requires an ability to function across racial and ethnic lines. White students who have sought out such experiences also represent a critical resource in successful multiracial communities.

Although more research needs to be done to discover the best way to identify applicants' multicultural leadership skills and cross-cultural learning aptitude, as a starting point we suggest the use of essay questions on college application forms. Wording such questions in a way that will be sensitive to students' concerns and will produce meaningful responses is no easy task. We offer the following sample questions only to illustrate the difficulty of the assignment and to provoke further thought and argument on the subject:

1. Describe an actual experience in which you observed or felt prejudice or discriminatory treatment based on race, ethnicity, gender, sexual orientation, or socioeconomic standing. Then comment on the situation, its causes, and its effects.
2. Describe an early experience from your own life of being a member of a minority—that is, a situation where you felt conspicuously different in some way from the majority of people in your group, school, neighborhood, or society. What did you take from that experience?
3. What are your expectations about relations among different racial and ethnic groups on campus? What do you think you will contribute to a multiracial college community?

Other evidence of students' ability to help create successful multiracial campuses might be found in letters of recommendation and in the course of personal interviews, provided that the forms and the interviewers ask the right questions.

Summary and Conclusion

It is now not only possible but necessary to consider college admissions criteria that evaluate applicants for their cross-cultural leadership potential in a multiethnic society. Such policies would, we hope, motivate elementary and secondary schools to place a higher priority on the cultivation of such skills. One way to accomplish this would be to ask questions on applications and in interviews that address issues of race and cultural identity inherent in multiethnic situations. We believe this would contribute to creating diverse college communities without having to rely on race-based admissions classifications.

References

Allport, G. W. (1979). *The nature of prejudice.* Cambridge, MA: Addison-Wesley. (Original work published 1954)

Astin, A. (1975). *Preventing students from dropping out.* San Francisco: Jossey-Bass.

Astin, A. (1993). Diversity and multiculturalism on campus: How are students affected? *Change, 25*(2), 44–49.

Duster, T. (1997, February). Unpublished speech given at the Pluralism and Unity conference, Hewlett Foundation, Millbrae, CA.

Murgia, E., Padilla, R., & Pavel, M. (1991). Ethnicity and the concept of social integration into Tinto's model of institutional departure. *Journal of College Student Development, 32.*

Tanaka, G. (1996a). Dysgenesis and white culture. In J. Kincheloe, S. Steinberg, & A. Gresson (Eds.), *Measured lies: The Bell Curve examined.* New York: St. Martin's Press.

Tanaka, G. (1996b). *The impact of multiculturalism on White students.* Unpublished doctoral dissertation, UCLA Graduate School of Education and Information Studies.

Tanaka, G. (1997). Pico College. In W. Tierney & Y. Lincoln (Eds.), *Representation and the text: Reframing the narrative voice.* Albany: State University of New York Press.

Notes

[1] "Student Enrollment in U.S. Higher Education Institutions by Race/Ethnicity, 1976–1994," *Digest of Education Statistics.* Washington, D.C.: National Center for Education Statistics, 1996.

[2] "Ethnic Group Percentages and Total Enrollments" (1979–1995), California Postsecondary Education Commission.

[3] These data derive from a larger study that began in 1994 with a qualitative pilot study (Tanaka, 1997) and was completed in 1996 using longitudinal survey results from 159 colleges and universities (Tanaka, 1996b). The 1985 freshmen survey and the 1989 follow-up from the Cooperative Institutional Research Program had generated over 25,000 responses from white students alone. To these data were added results from a 1989 survey of faculty at the same institutions. These data were subjected to a complex multiple regression analysis that examined the impact of various multicultural factors on four dependent variables. The two dependent variables we will focus on in this paper are "satisfaction with college" and "sense of community."

[4] Our measure of institutional priority was the faculty's mean response to the institutional goal, "to create a diverse multicultural environment."

[5] $p < .001$.

[6] In traditional statistical terminology, we identified an "interaction effect."

[7] $b = -.10$; this beta coefficient has a "p" value less than .001, meaning the finding is significant at the .001 level.

[8] $b = -.06$; this beta coefficient also has a "p" value less than .001.

About the Contributors

Alexander W. Astin holds the Allan M. Cartter Chair in Higher Education and Organizational Change at the University of California, Los Angeles.

Marguerite Bonous-Hammarth is Visiting Assistant Professor of Education at the University of California, Los Angeles.

Jorge Chapa is an Associate Professor in the Lyndon B. Johnson School of Public Affairs at the University of Texas, Austin.

Christopher Edley, Jr., is Professor of Law at Harvard Law School and Codirector of the Harvard Civil Rights Project.

Susanna Finnell is Executive Director of the Office of Honors Programs and Academic Scholarships at Texas A&M University.

Claire V. Handley serves as Assistant Director of Southern Education Foundation's program on Educational Opportunity and Postsecondary Education.

Thomas J. Kane is Associate Professor of Public Policy at the John F. Kennedy School of Government, Harvard University.

Jerome Karabel is Professor of Sociology at the University of California, Berkeley, and Codirector of the Berkeley Project on Equal Opportunity.

Robert A. Kronley is Senior Consultant to the BellSouth Foundation and to the Southern Education Foundation.

Vincent A. Lazaro is Director of Research at the Hispanic Association of Colleges and Universities.

Edward Miller, Coeditor of *Chilling Admissions,* has written widely on urban education and school reform. He is the former editor of the *Harvard Education Letter.*

Catherine M. Millett is a Senior Research Associate at the School of Education at the University of Michigan, and a Ph.D. candidate.

Michael T. Nettles is Professor of Education at the University of Michigan and Executive Director of the Frederick D. Patterson Research Institute of the United Negro College Fund.

Gary Orfield is Professor of Education and Social Policy at the Graduate School of Education and the John F. Kennedy School of Government, Harvard University. He is Codirector of the Harvard Civil Rights Project.

Laura W. Perna is Research Scientist and Director of Data Analyses at the Frederick D. Patterson Research Institute.

Greg Tanaka is a writer and lecturer.

Susan A. Wilbur is Director of Admissions and Relations with Schools at the University of California, Irvine.